vegan chocolate treats

60 Indulgent Sweets to Satisfy Your Inner Chocoholic

Ciarra Siller

creator of Peanut Butter Plus Chocolate

PAGE STREET
PUBLISHING CO.

PAGE STREET
PUBLISHING CO.

First published in 2020 by
Page Street Publishing Co.
27 Congress Street, Suite 105
Salem, MA 01970
www.pagestreetpublishing.com

Distributed by Macmillan, sales in Canada by The Canadian Manda Group.

24 23 22 21 20   1 2 3 4 5

ISBN-13: 978-1-64567-090-2
ISBN-10: 1-64567-090-2

Library of Congress Control Number: 2019957267

Cover and book design by Ashley Tenn for Page Street Publishing Co.
Photography by Ciarra Siller

Printed and bound in China

Dedication

To all my Peanut Butter Plus Chocolate followers and readers.
Thank you for your endless support!

Contents

Introduction

I grew up in a small town in southern Nevada, where my parents owned a custom furniture and antiques shop. If I wasn't building things with my dad, I was painting with my mom or writing and performing skits with my sister. My entire upbringing was centered around creativity, and I have my parents to thank for that.

I followed my creative instincts to Los Angeles to be an actor, bristling with excitement and brimming with optimism when I arrived. I love acting, but it's no secret that the business *around* acting is tough—and after years of juggling auditions, classes, plays and my "day job," I became burnt out and depressed. I was craving a creative outlet that I had control over.

I found solace in my sweet tooth. I've always loved chocolate—I owe that to my mom. If she and I had it our way, we would eat chocolate chip cookies for dinner. During some of my long nights rehearsing, I'm (only slightly) embarrassed to admit that that's exactly what I did.

These warm feelings generated inspiration, and it struck me unexpectedly one day. After an extended stretch of long hours in the theater, I finally had a day off and I was sitting in my small apartment in North Hollywood. For the first time in a long time, I was bored. I didn't have an audition or a class to go to, no one was calling me to cover a shift at the coffee shop—I was actually bored. So I decided to play around in the kitchen and baked some cookies using almond flour, peanut butter and oats. I snapped a quick photo on my phone and uploaded it to Instagram (this was 2011, when Instagram was just a fun, fledgling app and not the behemoth it is today). When I opened my Instagram a few hours later, I had comments from people I had never met asking me for the recipe.

For months, I continued to create dessert recipes in my spare time and to share them with my new visual audience. I quickly fell in love with finding the best light in my apartment to compose my photos, and before I knew it, I had purchased a used camera on eBay and taught myself how to use it. Peanut Butter Plus Chocolate was born, and it became an outlet for me—one that I finally had control over. It felt like freedom, and week after week, I couldn't wait to get back into the kitchen to create the next recipes to share.

Over the years, Peanut Butter Plus Chocolate has evolved into a recipe resource with not just chocolate recipes, but a variety of desserts—serving many different dietary needs. As I grow, so do my recipes. For health and ethical reasons, I do my best to eat mostly plants, and my recipes started to develop along with my dietary preferences. Not to mention that it has pushed me to challenge myself and my abilities. Creating recipes takes a lot of trial and error, testing and retesting and getting very creative. I thrive on new challenges, especially when chocolate is involved.

This book is the result of those challenges, and my hope is that it will help bring out your creativity in the kitchen too. Creating these recipes and writing this book have been the most rewarding and at times most challenging task of my life. My goal is for this book to be simple enough to be used by even the most novice of bakers—but with recipes that are as beautiful to serve as they are delicious. It is also important to me to include some gluten-free options so more people can enjoy this book—and the treats you create for your friends and family.

I have a secret dream that some of these recipes become your go-to treats when you are having that late-night chocolate craving, when you want to be the hit of your office party or when you just want to surprise a friend who needs a pick-me-up. I truly believe that baking and desserts bring people together, and my only wish is that this book does that for you.

Love,
Ciarra

Chocolate with a side of cookie

If you were to ask me what my favorite dessert in the whole world is, you might be surprised to hear my answer. I'm a simple girl who can be easily satisfied with a chocolate chip cookie. That's right, this simple classic will always be my favorite dessert. Chocolate chip cookies are a staple in my house for so many reasons: They're quick to make and not overly complicated, you can make a batch and freeze them to thaw and eat as you please and the best part is that they are travel-size! So naturally, cookies take their rightful place in the first chapter of this book. Here, you will find scrumptious cookies inspired by some of my favorite recipes, always with an extra twist of chocolate, like Brownie Snickerdoodle Cookies (page 10) and Cocoa-Swirled Meringue Cookies (page 29).

Brownie Snickerdoodle Cookies

This is really a brownie disguised as a cookie, with a soft and gooey chocolate center and rolled in cinnamon sugar. These cookies often remind me of Mexican hot chocolate. The cinnamon coating makes all the difference—it's a perfect complement to the delicious cocoa flavor.

Makes 16 cookies

DOUGH

1 tbsp (7 g) flax meal

3 tbsp (45 ml) water

1¼ cups (150 g) all-purpose flour

¼ cup (20 g) unsweetened cocoa powder

½ tsp baking soda

¼ tsp baking powder

⅛ tsp salt

½ cup (113 g) vegan butter, at room temperature

½ cup (100 g) granulated sugar

¼ cup (55 g) packed brown sugar

1 tsp vanilla extract

COATING

2 tbsp (24 g) granulated sugar

1 tsp ground cinnamon

Line a baking sheet with parchment paper.

To make the dough, in a small bowl, stir together the flax meal and water and then set it aside to gel for at least 5 minutes.

Meanwhile, in a mixing bowl, stir together the flour, cocoa powder, baking soda, baking powder and salt until combined.

In another bowl using an electric mixer, beat together the butter, granulated sugar and brown sugar until creamy, about 1 minute. Add the vanilla and the flax mixture and continue beating until well blended, about 1 minute. Add the wet ingredients to the dry ingredients and mix until a soft dough forms. Using a 1½-inch (3.8-cm) cookie scoop, make 16 evenly sized balls.

To make the coating, in a small bowl, stir together the granulated sugar and cinnamon. Roll each ball in the coating and place them on the baking sheet about 1 inch (2.5 cm) apart. Transfer the baking sheet to the freezer and chill for 10 minutes.

Preheat the oven to 350°F (180°C, or gas mark 4).

Remove the cookies from the freezer and bake them for 10 to 12 minutes, or until the edges are beginning to crisp. The centers will still be soft but will firm up as the cookies cool. Remove the cookies from the oven and let cool on a rack before serving.

The Most Amazing Chocolate Sugar Cookies (gf)

One of my favorite recipes from my blog is my Softest Gluten-Free Vegan Sugar Cookies, and it appears to be a fan favorite too! So I knew I had to make a chocolate version for this book. These are fun to make and fun to decorate with sprinkles.

Makes 24 cookies

DOUGH

1¾ cups (210 g) gluten-free baking flour

2 tbsp (18 g) arrowroot flour

¼ cup (20 g) unsweetened cocoa powder

½ tsp baking soda

⅛ tsp salt

½ cup (113 g) vegan butter, at room temperature

½ cup (100 g) granulated sugar

¼ cup (55 g) packed brown sugar

1 tsp vanilla extract

4 to 6 tbsp (60 to 90 ml) almond milk

CHOCOLATE BUTTERCREAM FROSTING

¼ cup (56 g) vegan butter, at room temperature

¼ cup (20 g) unsweetened cocoa powder, sifted

3 to 4 cups (345 to 460 g) confectioners' sugar, sifted, divided

¼ cup (60 ml) almond milk

1 tsp vanilla extract

Sprinkles, for decorating

Line two baking sheets with parchment paper.

To make the dough, in a large mixing bowl, sift together the gluten-free flour, arrowroot flour, cocoa powder, baking soda and salt and then set aside.

In another bowl using an electric mixer, beat together the butter, granulated sugar and brown sugar until creamy, about 1 minute. Add the vanilla and beat again. Add the dry ingredients to the wet ingredients and mix to combine, adding the almond milk, 1 tablespoon (15 ml) at a time, just until the dough comes together, and then don't add any more milk.

Shape the dough into a disk and place it between two pieces of parchment paper. With a rolling pin, roll out the dough to about ⅛ inch (3 mm) thick. Use your desired cookie cutters to cut out shapes and place them on the prepared baking sheets about 1 inch (2.5 cm) apart. Transfer the baking sheets to the freezer and chill for 10 minutes.

Preheat the oven to 350°F (180°C, or gas mark 4).

Remove the cookies from the freezer and bake them for 7 to 9 minutes, or until the edges begin to crisp. Let the cookies cool on the baking sheets for 5 minutes before transferring them to a cooling rack to cool completely.

To make the frosting, in a bowl using an electric mixer, beat the butter until creamy, about 1 minute. Add the cocoa powder and 1 cup (115 g) of the confectioners' sugar and mix until combined. Add the almond milk and vanilla and mix until smooth, about 30 seconds. Add the remaining 2 to 3 cups (230 to 345 g) of confectioners' sugar in 1-cup (115-g) increments until you reach a smooth but sturdy consistency. Decorate the cookies with the frosting and then immediately top with sprinkles before the frosting sets.

Double Fudge Chocolate Cookies

Chocolate lovers unite! These giant chocolate cookies with soft, velvety centers are impossible to resist. They're perfect with a glass of almond milk, so don't be shy about dipping and dunking!

Makes 10 cookies

1 tbsp (7 g) flax meal

3 tbsp (45 ml) water

1 cup (120 g) all-purpose flour

½ cup (60 g) cake flour

¼ cup (20 g) Dutch-processed cocoa powder

1½ tsp (5 g) tapioca flour

¾ tsp baking powder

½ tsp baking soda

⅛ tsp salt

½ cup (113 g) vegan butter, at room temperature

½ cup (110 g) packed brown sugar

¼ cup (50 g) granulated sugar

1 tsp vanilla extract

1 cup (180 g) vegan mini chocolate chips

Line two baking sheets with parchment paper.

In a small bowl, stir together the flax meal and water and then set it aside to gel for about 5 minutes. Meanwhile, in a mixing bowl, stir together the flours, cocoa powder, tapioca flour, baking powder, baking soda and salt until combined.

In another mixing bowl using an electric mixer, beat the butter, brown sugar and granulated sugar until light and fluffy, 1 to 2 minutes. Add the vanilla and the flax mixture and mix until combined. Slowly add the dry ingredients and mix until a dough forms. Fold in the chocolate chips. Divide the dough into 10 evenly sized balls and place them on the prepared baking sheets about 2 inches (5 cm) apart. Transfer the baking sheets to the freezer and chill for 1 hour.

Preheat the oven to 375°F (190°C, or gas mark 5).

Remove the cookies from the freezer and bake them for 14 to 16 minutes, or until the edges are beginning to crisp. The centers will still be soft but will firm up as the cookies cool. Let them cool for 10 minutes on the baking sheets before carefully transferring them to a rack to continue cooling.

Classic Chocolate Chunk Cookies

These are classic chocolate chunk cookies with soft centers, crispy edges and pools of chocolate, finished with flaky sea salt. They've been a go-to of mine for a long time, especially for gatherings and get-togethers—they never disappoint!

Makes 10 cookies

1 tbsp (7 g) flax meal

3 tbsp (45 ml) water

½ cup (113 g) vegan butter, at room temperature

½ cup (110 g) packed brown sugar

⅓ cup (68 g) granulated sugar

1½ cups (180 g) all-purpose flour

¾ tsp baking powder

½ tsp baking soda

24 oz (680 g) dark chocolate, chopped

Flaky sea salt

Preheat the oven to 350°F (180°C, or gas mark 4) with the rack in the center position. Line two baking sheets with parchment paper.

In a small bowl, stir together the flax meal and water and then set it aside to gel for about 5 minutes.

In a large bowl using an electric mixer, beat the butter until light and fluffy, 1 to 2 minutes, and then add the brown and granulated sugars and continue beating until smooth and creamy, about 1 minute. Add the flax mixture and beat to combine. Set aside.

In another mixing bowl, stir together the flour, baking powder and baking soda and then add half of it to the butter mixture and mix until combined. Add the remaining dry ingredients and mix until a dough forms and no dry spots remain, about 30 seconds. Add the chopped chocolate and mix until combined and evenly distributed.

Divide the dough into 10 evenly sized 3-inch (7.5-cm) balls. Place the balls on the prepared baking sheets 2 to 3 inches (5 to 7.5 cm) apart. I put 5 on each baking sheet. Bake the cookies for 8 minutes and then remove them from the oven and raise the center rack a few inches. Tap the cookie sheets against the counter a couple of times and then return them to the oven. Bake for 2 minutes, remove them from the oven and tap the baking sheets on the counter again to "deflate" the cookies and to spread the chocolate. Continue baking for 3 to 4 minutes longer, or until the edges start to brown.

Let the cookies cool on the baking sheets for 5 minutes before carefully transferring them to a rack to continue cooling. Sprinkle with flaky sea salt before serving.

Peanut Butter–Stuffed Chocolate Chip Cookies Dipped in Chocolate

Let's face it, nothing goes better with peanut butter than chocolate. This is such an everlasting truth that I named my blog after it: Peanut Butter Plus Chocolate. So as you can imagine, this is a cookie after my own heart.

Makes 12 cookies

12 dollops natural peanut butter

1 tbsp (7 g) flax meal

3 tbsp (45 ml) water

6 tbsp (84 g) vegan butter, at room temperature

½ cup (110 g) packed brown sugar

¼ cup (50 g) granulated sugar

1 tsp vanilla extract

1¾ cups (210 g) all-purpose flour

¾ tsp baking powder

½ tsp baking soda

1 cup (180 g) vegan mini chocolate chips, divided

½ tsp coconut oil

Flaky sea salt

Line two baking sheets with parchment paper. Place the dollops of peanut butter on one of the prepared baking sheets. Transfer the baking sheet to the freezer and chill until the peanut butter is solid, 4 to 5 minutes.

In a small bowl, stir together the flax meal and water and then set it aside to gel for about 5 minutes.

In a large bowl using an electric mixer, beat the butter and both sugars until smooth and creamy, 1 to 2 minutes. Add the vanilla and flax mixture and beat until well combined, about 1 minute.

In another bowl, stir together the flour, baking powder, baking soda and ½ cup (90 g) of the chocolate chips. Add the dry ingredients to the wet ingredients and stir with a rubber spatula just until a dough forms. Divide the dough into 12 evenly sized balls and place on the second prepared baking sheet.

Remove the peanut butter from the freezer. Take one of the cookie dough balls and press it into a flat disk. Place one of the solid peanut butter dollops in the center of the cookie dough and then roll the cookie dough back up into a ball so it seals the peanut butter inside completely. Place the peanut butter–stuffed balls 2 inches (5 cm) apart on both prepared baking sheets and return them to the freezer for 15 minutes.

Preheat the oven to 350°F (180°C, or gas mark 4).

Remove the cookies from the freezer and bake them for 10 to 12 minutes, until the edges are golden brown. Let them cool on the baking sheets for 5 minutes before transferring the cookies to a rack to continue cooling.

In a small, microwave-safe bowl, melt together the remaining ½ cup (90 g) of chocolate chips and the coconut oil on 50 percent power until smooth. Dip each cookie halfway into the chocolate. Place the dipped cookies on a cooling rack and let the chocolate harden at room temperature. Sprinkle with flaky sea salt before serving.

Life-Changing Oatmeal Walnut Cookies

Huge oatmeal cookie fan here! Maybe you are too? It might be an unpopular opinion, but I am not a fan of raisins in my oatmeal cookies. Simple fix—chocolate to the rescue (proving that chocolate never lets you down)! Did you expect anything different from this cookbook?

Makes 18 cookies

1 tbsp (7 g) flax meal

3 tbsp (45 ml) water

½ cup (113 g) vegan butter, at room temperature

½ cup (110 g) packed brown sugar

½ cup (100 g) granulated sugar

1 tsp vanilla extract

1½ cups (135 g) rolled oats

¾ cup plus 3 tbsp (115 g) all-purpose flour

1 tbsp (9 g) tapioca flour

½ tsp baking soda

¾ cup (80 g) walnuts, chopped

3 oz (84 g) vegan chocolate, chopped

Flaky sea salt

Line a baking sheet with parchment paper.

In a small bowl, stir together the flax meal and water and then set it aside to gel, about 5 minutes.

In a large bowl using an electric mixer, beat together the butter and both sugars until smooth and creamy, 1 to 2 minutes. Add the vanilla and flax mixture and beat until well combined, about 1 minute.

In another bowl, stir together the rolled oats, all-purpose flour, tapioca flour, baking soda, walnuts and chocolate. Add the dry ingredients to the wet ingredients and stir with a rubber spatula just until a dough forms. Divide the dough into 18 balls using a 2-inch (5-cm) cookie scoop and place them on the prepared baking sheet about 2 inches (5 cm) apart. Transfer the baking sheet to the freezer and chill for at least 30 minutes.

Preheat the oven to 350°F (180°C, or gas mark 4).

Remove the cookies from the freezer and bake them for 12 to 14 minutes, until the edges are golden brown. Let them cool on the baking sheet for 5 minutes before transferring the cookies to a rack to continue cooling. Sprinkle with flaky sea salt before serving.

Note: To emphasize the chocolate in the presentation, add chocolate chunks to the tops of the cookies (I like to stick them where the cracks naturally form) just as they come out of the oven.

Soft and Chewy Brownie-Swirled Cookies

These cookies are perfect for days when you can't choose between crackly chocolate brownies and classic chocolate chip cookies—a typical day for me. Get the best of both worlds with these chewy chocolate chip brownie cookies, a.k.a. "brookies." The secret to these cookies is to not overbake them. Cookies continue to cook when removed from the oven, so 10 to 12 minutes is just enough time!

Makes 22 cookies

CHOCOLATE CHIP COOKIE DOUGH

1 tbsp (7 g) flax meal

3 tbsp (45 ml) water

1¼ cups (150 g) all-purpose flour

1 tsp baking soda

1 cup (180 g) vegan chocolate chips

6 tbsp (85 g) vegan butter, at room temperature

⅓ cup (75 g) packed brown sugar

¼ cup (50 g) granulated sugar

1 tsp vanilla extract

BROWNIE BATTER

1 tbsp (7 g) flax meal

3 tbsp (45 ml) water

1 cup (120 g) all-purpose flour

¼ cup (20 g) unsweetened cocoa powder

1 tsp baking soda

½ cup (90 g) vegan chocolate chips

5 tbsp (75 g) vegan butter, at room temperature

⅓ cup (75 g) packed brown sugar

⅓ cup (68 g) granulated sugar

1 tsp vanilla extract

Flaky sea salt

Preheat the oven to 350°F (180°C, or gas mark 4) and line two baking sheets with parchment paper.

To make the chocolate chip cookie dough, in a small bowl, stir together the flax meal and water and then set it aside to gel, about 5 minutes.

In a medium bowl, stir together the flour, baking soda and chocolate chips.

In a large bowl using an electric mixer, beat the butter until light and fluffy, 1 to 2 minutes. Add the brown sugar, granulated sugar and vanilla and beat until smooth and creamy, about 1 minute. Add the flax mixture and stir until well combined. Add the dry ingredients to the wet ingredients and mix with a rubber spatula until a dough forms, about 1 minute. Set this dough aside while you prepare the brownies.

To make the brownie batter, in a small bowl, stir together the flax meal and water and then set it aside to gel, about 5 minutes.

In a medium bowl, stir together the flour, cocoa powder, baking soda and chocolate chips.

In a large bowl using an electric mixer, beat the butter until light and fluffy, 1 to 2 minutes. Add the brown sugar, granulated sugar and vanilla and beat until creamy, about 1 minute. Add the flax mixture and beat until combined. Add the dry ingredients to the wet ingredients and mix with a rubber spatula until a dough forms, about 1 minute.

Divide both doughs into 22 evenly sized pieces (about 1½ teaspoons [8 g]) and roll them into balls. Take one chocolate chip cookie dough ball and one brownie dough ball and roll them together to make one ball. Place the brownie-cookie on the prepared baking sheets, spacing them about 1½ inches (3.8 cm) apart. Bake them for 10 to 12 minutes, until the edges are beginning to crisp. The centers will still be soft but will firm up as the cookies cool. Remove the baking sheets from the oven and let the cookies cool on the pan for 5 minutes before transferring them to a wire rack to continue cooling for 15 minutes. Sprinkle them with sea salt before serving.

Super Soft Homemade Oreos

Inspired by my favorite cookie of all time, these homemade Oreos are super soft, unlike their popular counterpart. They are more like a heavenly cream filling sandwiched by two rich chocolate brownies—either way, these cookies are insanely delicious!

Makes 10 cookies

COOKIES

1 tbsp (7 g) flax meal

3 tbsp (45 ml) water

1½ cups (180 g) all-purpose flour

10 tbsp (50 g) Dutch-processed cocoa powder

1 tsp baking soda

½ tsp baking powder

⅛ tsp sea salt

½ cup (113 g) vegan butter, at room temperature

¾ cup (150 g) granulated sugar

¼ cup (55 g) packed brown sugar

2 tsp (10 ml) vanilla extract

FILLING

¼ cup (56 g) vegan shortening

2 tbsp (28 g) vegan butter, at room temperature

1¼ to 2 cups (150 to 230 g) confectioners' sugar, sifted

Preheat the oven to 350°F (180°C, or gas mark 4) and line two baking sheets with parchment paper.

To make the cookies, in a small bowl, stir together the flax meal and water and then set it aside to gel, about 5 minutes.

In a medium bowl, stir together the flour, cocoa powder, baking soda, baking powder and salt.

In a large bowl using an electric mixer, beat the butter, granulated sugar and brown sugar until light and fluffy, 1 to 2 minutes. Add the vanilla and flax mixture and beat until well combined, about 1 minute. Slowly add the dry ingredients to the wet ingredients and mix with a rubber spatula until a dough forms, about 1 minute.

Divide the dough into 20 evenly sized balls. Place them on the prepared baking sheets about 2 inches (5 cm) apart and press them down about halfway. Bake them for 7 to 8 minutes, until the edges darken. Let them cool on the baking sheet for 5 minutes before carefully transferring them to a rack to continue cooling, for 15 to 20 minutes.

To make the filling, in a bowl using an electric mixer, beat the shortening and butter until smooth, 1 to 2 minutes. Add the confectioners' sugar about ¼ cup (30 g) at a time and beat until the filling is sturdy but pliable.

Spread the bottom of 10 cookies with the filling and place another cookie, bottom side down, on top. Press lightly to spread the filling to the edges.

Copycat Levain Chocolate Chip Cookies

If you haven't visited Levain Bakery in New York City, chances are that you have heard of it and their epic cookies because they are just that—EPIC! The first time I tried these cookies was about fourteen years ago on a school trip, and I swear I haven't stopped thinking about them since. Levain Bakery cookies are tennis ball–size mounds with perfectly crisp edges and gooey centers. Although no one knows Levain Bakery's secrets to keeping their colossal shape, these chocolate chip walnut cookies are the perfect, if slightly smaller, vegan copycat.

Makes 7 cookies

1 tbsp (7 g) flax meal

3 tbsp (45 ml) water

1 cup (120 g) cake flour

¾ cup (90 g) all-purpose flour

2 tbsp (18 g) tapioca flour

1 tsp baking powder

½ tsp baking soda

⅛ tsp sea salt

½ cup (113 g) vegan butter, at room temperature

½ cup (110 g) packed brown sugar

¼ cup (50 g) granulated sugar

1 tsp vanilla extract

1 cup (180 g) mini vegan chocolate chips

1 cup (112 g) walnuts, chopped

Line two baking sheets with parchment paper.

In a small bowl, stir together the flax meal and water and then set it aside to gel, about 5 minutes.

In a medium bowl, stir together the flours, baking powder, baking soda and salt.

In a large bowl using an electric mixer, beat together the butter, brown sugar and granulated sugar until light and fluffy, 1 to 2 minutes. Add the vanilla and flax mixture and beat until well combined. Slowly add the dry ingredients and mix with a rubber spatula just until a dough forms, about 1 minute. Fold in the chocolate chips and chopped walnuts.

Divide the dough into 7 evenly sized balls (about the size of golf balls) and place them on the prepared baking sheets at least 2 inches (5 cm) apart. Transfer the baking sheet to the freezer and chill for at least 2 hours.

Preheat the oven to 375°F (190°C, or gas mark 5).

Remove the baking sheets from the freezer and bake the cookies for 15 to 17 minutes, or until the edges are golden brown. Let the cookies cool on the baking sheets for 10 minutes before transferring them to a rack to continue cooling.

Cocoa-Swirled Meringue Cookies 🅶🅵

Aquafaba (the liquid from a can of chickpeas) might be the most magical ingredient of all time—it works just like egg whites! It's hard to believe this magical liquid can produce such light and crispy cookies, but it does!

Makes 20 to 30 cookies

¾ cup (180 ml) aquafaba

¼ tsp cream of tartar

⅔ cup (135 g) granulated sugar

2 tbsp (10 g) unsweetened cocoa powder, sifted

½ cup (90 g) chopped vegan chocolate

1 tsp coconut oil

Preheat the oven to 210°F (100°C) and place the rack in the middle position. Line two baking sheets with parchment paper.

In a large glass mixing bowl using an electric mixer, or in a standing mixer with the whisk attachment, beat the aquafaba on medium speed until frothy, about 2 minutes. Add the cream of tartar and beat on high speed for 4 to 6 minutes, or until stiff peaks form.

While still beating on high, add the sugar 1 tablespoon (12 g) at a time. Once you have added all the sugar, the mixture should be glossy. Beat for 1 to 2 minutes longer, and then turn off the mixer. Add the sifted cocoa powder and use a rubber spatula to fold the meringue in just four turns to keep the swirl of cocoa in place.

Fit a piping bag with a plain or star tip. Unfold the top of the piping bag and use the spatula to fill the bag with meringue. Pipe meringue kisses onto the baking sheets, fitting as many as you can on one baking sheet while also leaving about ½ inch (1.3 cm) of space in between each one.

Bake the meringues for 75 minutes or until they are dry to the touch, and then turn off the oven and crack open the door. Leave the meringues in the oven for 20 minutes while the oven cools. Once the meringues are cooled, they should peel off the parchment paper easily.

In a small, microwave-safe bowl, melt together the chocolate and coconut oil on 50 percent power until smooth. Dip the bottom of each meringue in the chocolate and swirl it around so the excess drips off, then return it to the parchment paper. Repeat until you have dipped each meringue in chocolate. Let the chocolate harden before serving.

Brownies, fudge and bars, oh my!

Nothing lifts my spirits quite like a layered dessert. Perhaps that's what I love most about brownies, fudge and bars—the way you can customize the layers to fit a dessert *inside another dessert*! Endless possibilities led to hundreds of ideas, and it was no small task to narrow it down to the selections you find here. This chapter contains some of the most decadent chocolate sweets in the book, such as my Frosted Cookies and Cream Brownies (page 39) and Magical Millionaire Bars (page 36).

Chocolate Chip Cookie Skillet Brownie

Skip the plates. Just grab a fork and dig in—this dessert is fun for sharing with a small group of friends or family. Gooey cookie centers are layered with brownie and chocolate chips. My favorite way to enjoy this is with a scoop or two of dairy-free ice cream on top!

Serves 6

1 tbsp (7 g) flax meal
3 tbsp (45 ml) water

COOKIE LAYER

½ cup (60 g) all-purpose flour
½ tsp baking soda
⅓ cup (60 g) vegan chocolate chips
3 tbsp (42 g) vegan butter, at room temperature
3 tbsp (42 g) packed brown sugar
2 tbsp (24 g) granulated sugar
1 tsp vanilla extract

BROWNIE LAYER

6 tbsp (48 g) all-purpose flour
2 tbsp (10 g) unsweetened cocoa powder
½ tsp baking soda
2½ tbsp (35 g) vegan butter, at room temperature
3 tbsp (42 g) packed brown sugar
2 tbsp (24 g) granulated sugar
1 tsp vanilla extract

TOPPINGS

Chopped chocolate
Mini pretzels
Vegan ice cream (optional)

Preheat the oven to 350°F (180°C, or gas mark 4) and coat an 8- to 10-inch (20- to 25-cm) oven-safe skillet with vegan butter or nonstick spray.

In a small bowl, stir together the flax meal and water and then set it aside to gel, about 5 minutes.

To make the cookie layer, in a medium bowl, stir together the flour, baking soda and chocolate chips.

In a large bowl using an electric mixer, beat the butter, brown sugar and granulated sugar until creamy, 1 to 2 minutes. Add the vanilla and half of the flax mixture and beat until well combined, about 1 minute. Add the dry ingredients and mix with a rubber spatula until a dough forms, about 1 minute. Use the rubber spatula to spread the cookie dough on the bottom of the prepared skillet; set aside.

To make the brownie layer, in the same bowl you mixed the cookie layer's dry ingredients, stir together the flour, cocoa powder and baking soda.

In a large bowl using an electric mixer, beat the butter, brown sugar and granulated sugar until creamy, 1 to 2 minutes. Add the vanilla and the remaining half of the flax mixture from the cookie layer and beat until well combined, about 1 minute. Add the dry ingredients and mix with a rubber spatula until a dough forms, about 1 minute. Use the rubber spatula to spread the brownie layer over the cookie layer.

Place the skillet in the oven and bake for 10 minutes. Remove the skillet and top the brownie with the chocolate and pretzels, and then return it to the oven and bake for 10 to 12 minutes longer, until the edges are beginning to crisp. The centers will still be soft but will firm up as the cookie skillet cools. Let cool for 10 minutes before serving. Top with ice cream, if desired.

Delicious Walnut Fudge (gf)

I have been making fudge for years. Growing up, I remember my aunt would make the sweetest and creamiest chocolate fudge during the holidays and she would often let me help her in the kitchen. It's so simple to make, requires very few ingredients (yay!) and the best part is that once it's made it can last for a couple of weeks in the refrigerator. I added walnuts for extra texture, but if you prefer a smooth fudge, they can be omitted or replaced with your favorite nut!

Makes 32 pieces

1 (11.6-oz [330-g]) can sweetened condensed coconut milk

2 cups (360 g) vegan dark chocolate chips

1 tsp vanilla extract

⅛ tsp sea salt

½ cup (60 g) walnuts, chopped

1 tbsp (5 g) Dutch-processed cocoa powder

Coat an 8 x 4–inch (20 x 10–cm) or similar size loaf pan with nonstick spray, and then line it with parchment paper, leaving an overhang so you can easily remove the fudge.

In a small pot, combine the condensed coconut milk and chocolate chips and cook over medium-low heat, stirring almost continuously, until the chocolate is melted and smooth, 3 to 4 minutes. Remove the pot from the heat and stir in the vanilla, salt and walnuts.

Scrape the mixture into the prepared pan and press it evenly along the bottom. Place the fudge in the freezer for 20 to 30 minutes, or until solid.

Use the parchment-paper handles to remove the block of fudge from the pan. Dust the top of the fudge with the cocoa powder and then cut it into 32 (1-inch [2.5-cm]) squares.

Magical Millionaire Bars gf

This gluten-free dessert has three layers: shortbread crust, date caramel and decadent chocolate. I like working with layers, not just because it's fun cooking but also because I love the end result: With every bite you get a bit of crumbly shortbread, gooey caramel and decadent chocolate all contributing to the deliciousness!

Makes 20 bars

CRUST

1½ cups (168 g) packed almond flour

¼ cup (36 g) arrowroot flour

¼ tsp salt

3 tbsp (45 g) coconut oil, melted

2 tbsp (30 ml) maple syrup

CARAMEL

¼ cup (64 g) cashew butter

20 soft Medjool dates, pitted and chopped

⅛ tsp salt

2 tbsp (30 ml) water

CHOCOLATE

1 cup (180 g) vegan chocolate chips

1 tbsp (14 g) coconut oil

Flaky sea salt

Preheat the oven to 350°F (180°C, or gas mark 4). Line an 8 x 8–inch (20 x 20–cm) pan with parchment paper, leaving an overhang so you can easily remove the bars.

To make the crust, in a medium bowl, stir together the almond flour, arrowroot flour and salt. Add the coconut oil and maple syrup and use a fork to stir the ingredients together until combined. Press the mixture into the bottom of the prepared pan and bake the crust for 9 to 11 minutes, or until the edges are golden brown. Remove the pan from the oven and let the crust cool in the pan.

To make the caramel, add the cashew butter, dates and salt to a food processor and process on high speed for 1 minute, or until the mixture begins to form a ball. Add the water and continue blending until smooth and incorporated, about 15 seconds. You may need to stop and scrape the sides from time to time.

Carefully spread the caramel layer over the crust using a rubber spatula. If the caramel is too sticky, wet your fingertips and then use your hands to evenly press the caramel over the crust. Place the pan in the freezer to chill while you make the chocolate.

To make the chocolate, in a microwave-safe bowl, melt together the chocolate chips and coconut oil on 50 percent power until smooth, 1 to 2 minutes. Stop every 45 seconds and stir. Once the chocolate is smooth, remove the pan from the freezer and pour the chocolate over the caramel layer. Cover the pan with plastic wrap and chill in the refrigerator for 30 minutes.

Use the parchment-paper handles to remove the block of bars from the pan. Sprinkle the top with flaky sea salt and cut into 20 bars.

Frosted Cookies and Cream Brownies

My love for Oreos runs deep, and so does my love for brownies, so combining the two was a no-brainer. These are a little different from traditional brownies, and they always get great reviews when I share them with friends.

Makes 16 brownies

BROWNIES

2 tbsp (14 g) flax meal

5 tbsp (75 ml) water

1 cup (180 g) vegan chocolate chips

6 tbsp (84 g) vegan butter

¾ cup (165 g) packed brown sugar

1 tsp vanilla extract

1 cup plus 2 tbsp (136 g) all-purpose flour

¼ tsp baking soda

GANACHE

1 cup (180 g) vegan chocolate chips

¼ cup (60 ml) almond milk

8 double-stuffed chocolate sandwich cookies (116 g) (I recommend Double-Stuf Oreos), crushed

Preheat the oven to 350°F (180°C, or gas mark 4) and line an 8 x 8–inch (20 x 20–cm) pan with parchment paper, leaving an overhang so you can easily remove the brownies.

To make the brownies, in a small bowl, stir together the flax meal and water, and then set it aside to gel for at least 5 minutes.

In a large, microwave-safe bowl, melt together the chocolate chips and butter on 50 percent power for 30 to 50 seconds, and then stir until it's smooth. Whisk in the brown sugar and vanilla until smooth. Add the flax mixture and stir until well combined. Fold in the flour and baking soda until no dry spots remain.

Transfer the batter to the prepared pan and press it evenly into the bottom. Bake the brownies for 16 to 18 minutes. The center should still be soft, but a crust layer will have formed over the top. Let the brownies cool before preparing the ganache.

To make the ganache, in a microwave-safe bowl, melt together the chocolate chips and almond milk on 50 percent power in 30-second increments, stirring in between, until smooth. Pour the ganache over the cooled brownies and smooth with a knife. Top with the crushed cookies and chill until the chocolate is set, about 1 hour in the refrigerator or, if you can't wait to eat them, 15 minutes in the freezer will do. Use the parchment-paper handles to remove the block of brownies from the pan and cut into 16 pieces.

Almond Butter Swirl Brownies

These fudgy, decadent brownies are topped with a chocolate ganache and almond butter swirl. These come out looking like they took a lot more effort, but in fact this is a really simple recipe with a short list of ingredients.

Makes 16 brownies

BROWNIES

1¼ cups (340 g) natural almond butter

¾ cup (180 ml) maple syrup

¾ cup (60 g) unsweetened cocoa powder

¼ cup (30 g) all-purpose flour

½ tsp baking soda

¼ tsp salt

TOPPING

1 cup (180 g) vegan chocolate chips

1 tbsp (14 g) coconut oil

¼ cup (68 g) almond butter

Preheat the oven to 350°F (180°C, or gas mark 4) and prepare an 8 x 8-inch (20 x 20–cm) pan with parchment paper, leaving an overhang so you can easily remove the brownies.

To make the brownies, in a large mixing bowl, stir together the almond butter, maple syrup and cocoa powder until smooth, about 1 minute. Add the flour, baking soda and salt and stir until a dough forms. Press the dough evenly into the bottom of the prepared pan. Bake the brownies for 17 to 20 minutes, until the edges are beginning to crisp. The centers will still be soft but will firm up as the cookies cool. Remove the pan from the oven and let cool for 15 minutes.

To make the topping, in a microwave-safe bowl, melt the chocolate and coconut oil on 50 percent power for 1 to 2 minutes. Stop every 45 seconds and stir. Once smooth, pour the chocolate over the brownies. Drop teaspoon-size dollops of almond butter over the chocolate and use a sharp knife to swirl the almond butter and chocolate together. Chill in the refrigerator until the chocolate is solid, about 20 minutes. Use the parchment-paper handles to remove the block of brownies from the pan and cut into 16 pieces.

Note: For a gluten-free brownie, substitute the all-purpose flour for an all-purpose gluten-free flour, such as Bob's Red Mill Gluten Free 1 to 1 Baking Flour.

No-Bake Dark Chocolate Peanut Butter Bars **gf**

One of my favorite holiday cookies growing up were buckeye peanut butter balls—this is quite possibly where my love for chocolate and peanut butter began. These No-Bake Dark Chocolate Peanut Butter Bars reimagine the classic buckeye balls from my youth—only bigger and square.

Makes 16 bars

½ cup (113 g) vegan butter, at room temperature

1¾ cups (440 g) natural peanut butter

10 tbsp (80 g) coconut flour, plus more as needed

1 cup (180 g) vegan dark chocolate chips

1 tbsp (14 g) coconut oil

Line an 8 x 8–inch (20 x 20–cm) pan with parchment paper, leaving an overhang so you can easily remove the brownies.

In a large mixing bowl with an electric mixer, beat the butter until light and fluffy, about 1 minute. Add the peanut butter and mix until smooth. Add the coconut flour and mix until a dough forms. The dough should be dry enough that it doesn't stick to the bowl but not so dry that it's stiff. Add more coconut flour if necessary. Press the dough evenly into the bottom of the pan using a rubber spatula.

In a microwave-safe bowl, melt together the chocolate chips and coconut oil on 50 percent power in 30-second increments, stirring in between, until smooth. Pour the chocolate over the peanut butter layer and use a rubber spatula to smooth the top. Chill in the freezer for 10 to 15 minutes. Use the parchment-paper handles to remove the block of bars from the pan and cut into 16 bars.

Note: Store the bars in the refrigerator—they are delicious cold!

S'mores Brownies

The two best desserts mashed up into one indulgent treat. No campfire needed, although the toasted marshmallows will certainly remind you of summer cookouts with friends!

Makes 16 brownies

CRUST

5 oz (140 g) graham crackers

¼ cup (56 g) vegan butter, melted

BROWNIES

2 tbsp (14 g) flax meal

6 tbsp (90 ml) water

1 cup (180 g) vegan chocolate chips

½ cup (113 g) vegan butter

¾ cup (165 g) packed brown sugar

1 tsp vanilla extract

1 cup (120 g) all-purpose flour

¼ tsp baking soda

⅛ tsp salt

TOPPING

¼ cup (40 g) chopped vegan chocolate

16 vegan marshmallows

Preheat the oven to 350°F (180°C, or gas mark 4) and line an 8 x 8–inch (20 x 20–cm) pan with parchment paper, leaving an overhang so you can easily remove the brownies.

To make the crust, place the graham crackers in a food processor or blender and blend until fine crumbs form. Add the melted butter and blend until incorporated. Press the mixture into the bottom of the prepared pan and bake the crust for 6 to 8 minutes, until golden brown. Be careful not to overbake. Remove from the oven and let the crust cool.

To make the brownies, in a small bowl, stir together the flax meal and water and then set it aside to gel for about 5 minutes.

In a large, microwave-safe bowl, melt together the chocolate chips and butter on 50 percent power in 20-second increments, stirring in between, until smooth. Whisk in the brown sugar and vanilla until incorporated. Add the flax mixture and stir until well combined.

Sift the flour, baking soda and salt on top of the chocolate mixture and fold the mixture together until a batter forms. Pour the batter over the baked crust and return the pan to the oven to bake the brownies for 24 to 26 minutes, until the edges are beginning to darken and crisp. The centers will still be soft but will firm up as the cookies cool.

For the topping, remove the brownies from the oven, sprinkle the top with the chopped chocolate and let it sit for 15 minutes.

Cut the marshmallows in half so you have 32 equal pieces and place them over the chocolate, which should now be melted. Use a kitchen torch to gently toast the marshmallows, or turn the oven to high broil and toast the marshmallows for 1 to 2 minutes, being careful not to burn them! Use the parchment-paper handles to remove the block of brownies from the pan and cut into 16 pieces.

Cookie Dough Chocolate Bars

Cookie dough always reminds me of my mom. Chocolate chip cookies rarely got to the baking stage in my house when I was growing up, because Mom taught me at a young age that cookie dough will always be the ultimate treat. My recipe takes the extra step of heat-treating the flour, so the dough is 100 percent safe to eat.

Makes 12 pieces

COOKIE DOUGH

½ cup (113 g) vegan butter, at room temperature

⅓ cup (68 g) granulated sugar

⅓ cup (75 g) packed brown sugar

3 tbsp (45 ml) almond milk

1 tsp vanilla extract

1¼ cups (150 g) all-purpose flour or gluten-free baking flour, heat-treated (see Note)

½ cup (90 g) mini vegan chocolate chips

TOPPING

2 cups (360 g) vegan chocolate chips, for dipping

Have ready two 9 x 5–inch (23 x 13–cm) silicone chocolate molds. If you don't have molds, line a 9 x 5–inch (23 x 13–cm) baking pan with parchment paper, leaving an overhang so you can easily remove the bars.

To make the cookie dough, in a large bowl using an electric mixer, beat together the butter, granulated sugar and brown sugar until smooth and creamy, about 1 minute. Add the almond milk and vanilla and beat until combined, about 1 minute. Stir in the flour and mini chocolate chips. Press half of the cookie dough evenly into the bottom of each mold or into the bottom of the pan.

To make the topping, in a microwave-safe bowl, melt the chocolate chips on 50 percent power for 1 to 2 minutes, or until the chocolate is melted, stirring occasionally. Pour the chocolate over the cookie dough and chill in the freezer for 15 to 20 minutes. Pop the bars out of the molds or use the parchment-paper handles to remove the block of bars from the pan and cut into 12 pieces. Store the bars in the refrigerator.

Note: To heat-treat the flour, preheat the oven to 350°F (180°C, or gas mark 4) and spread the flour in an even layer on a baking sheet. Bake for 10 minutes. Let the flour cool and sift it before using.

Chocolate Fudge Coconut Crumb Bars

Desserts in the form of bars are my favorite! I don't know why, but maybe it's because sharp angles are more appealing to the eye? Or maybe it's because all of my square desserts are made with chocolate, like these fudge-filled gluten-free coconut crumb bars.

Makes 20 bars

CRUST

2 cups (240 g) gluten-free baking flour

½ cup (40 g) Dutch-processed cocoa powder

½ cup (42 g) unsweetened coconut flakes

½ cup (100 g) granulated sugar

⅛ tsp salt

¾ cup (168 g) vegan butter, melted

FUDGE

1 (11.6-oz [330-g]) can sweetened condensed coconut milk

2 cups (360 g) chopped vegan dark chocolate

Preheat the oven to 350°F (180°C, or gas mark 4) and line an 8 x 8–inch (20 x 20–cm) pan with parchment paper, leaving an overhang so you can easily remove the bars.

To make the crust, in a mixing bowl, stir together the flour, cocoa powder, coconut flakes, sugar and salt. Add the melted butter and stir, using a fork until crumbles form. Pour two-thirds of the mixture into the bottom of the prepared pan and pack it tightly using the bottom of a glass. Refrigerate the remaining crumbles. Bake the crust for 6 to 7 minutes, until darkened in color. The crust will set as it cools. Remove the pan from the oven and let the crust cool.

To make the fudge, combine the condensed coconut milk and chocolate in a heatproof glass bowl over a small pot of water and set the burner to medium-low heat. Melt the chocolate, stirring, until smooth, 4 to 5 minutes. Pour the fudge into the crust and top with the remaining crumbles. Press the crumbles into the fudge layer. Cover the pan with plastic wrap and chill in the refrigerator for at least 2 hours. Use the parchment-paper handles to remove the block of bars from the pan and cut into 20 pieces.

Have your
cake and pie it, too

Baking cakes and pies always comes with a certain satisfaction. The end result can feel like a masterpiece. Not to mention that you get to eat said masterpiece. My favorite part though? I've always enjoyed the cake-making process because frosting a cake to perfection is therapeutic AF! The cakes and pies in this chapter are bursting with loads of chocolate to help you create your own masterpiece, such as Double Chocolate Cream Pie (page 60) or Death by Chocolate Blackout Cake (page 52). I promise this chapter will be the most fun one in the book. If you don't believe me now, you will just have to see for yourself!

Death by Chocolate Blackout Cake

A pure classic. Decadent dark chocolate cake filled with chocolate chips and layered with chocolate buttercream, this cake is straight from the depths of my most chocolatey dreams.

Serves 10

CAKE

2 cups (240 g) all-purpose flour

⅔ cup (55 g) Dutch-processed cocoa powder

2 tsp (6 g) baking soda

½ tsp sea salt

½ cup (90 g) vegan chocolate chips

½ cup (120 g) coconut oil, melted

⅔ cup (148 g) packed brown sugar

⅔ cup (135 g) granulated sugar

1½ cups (360 ml) almond milk, at room temperature

¼ cup (60 g) applesauce, at room temperature

2 tsp (10 ml) vanilla extract

2 tbsp (30 ml) distilled white vinegar

FROSTING

1 cup (226 g) vegan butter, at room temperature

¼ cup (56 g) vegan shortening

½ cup (40 g) Dutch-processed cocoa powder

3½ cups (400 g) confectioners' sugar

2 tbsp (30 ml) almond milk

2 tsp (10 ml) vanilla extract

¼ cup (40 g) mini vegan chocolate chips

Preheat the oven to 350°F (180°C, or gas mark 4) and coat two 6-inch (15-cm) round pans with nonstick spray, and then line the bottom with parchment paper.

To make the cake, in a large bowl, stir together the flour, cocoa powder, baking soda, salt and chocolate chips until combined.

In another bowl with an electric mixer, beat together the coconut oil, brown sugar and granulated sugar until combined, about 30 seconds. Add the almond milk, applesauce and vanilla and beat until combined, about 30 seconds. Stir in the vinegar. The mixture will separate a bit and that's okay. Add the dry ingredients to the wet and stir with a rubber spatula until a batter forms. Divide the batter between the prepared cake pans and bake them for 30 to 35 minutes, until a toothpick inserted into the center comes out clean. Remove the pans from the oven and let the cakes cool completely. Turn them out of the pans and peel off the parchment paper.

To make the frosting, in a large bowl with an electric mixer, beat together the butter and shortening until smooth and fluffy, 1 to 2 minutes. Add the cocoa powder and beat until combined. Add the confectioners' sugar, 1 cup (115 g) at a time, and beat until incorporated. Add the almond milk and vanilla and beat until smooth.

Frost the top of one cake, place the other cake on top and frost the top of that cake and the sides of the entire cake. Decorate with the mini chocolate chips.

Raspberry Chocolate Bundt Cake

As much as I love creating beautiful layered cakes, it's the simplicity of a Bundt cake that I enjoy most. This chocolate Bundt cake is filled with raspberries and topped with a decadent chocolate glaze. The slight tartness from the raspberries is nicely infused into the cake—these are flavors that go so well together!

Serves 10

CAKE

3 cups (360 g) all-purpose flour

1 cup (200 g) granulated sugar

2 tsp (6 g) baking powder

1½ tsp (4 g) baking soda

¾ tsp salt

1 cup (240 ml) almond milk, at room temperature

½ cup (120 g) coconut oil, melted

1 tbsp (15 ml) distilled white vinegar

1 tsp vanilla extract

1½ cups (185 g) fresh raspberries

CHOCOLATE GLAZE

½ cup (90 g) chopped vegan chocolate

1 tsp coconut oil

Preheat the oven to 350°F (180°C, or gas mark 4). Generously coat a Bundt pan with nonstick spray.

To make the cake, in a large bowl, whisk together the flour, sugar, baking powder, baking soda and salt until combined.

In a medium bowl, whisk together the almond milk, coconut oil, vinegar and vanilla until smooth. Add the wet ingredients to the dry ingredients and stir with a rubber spatula until a batter forms and no dry spots remain. Fold in the raspberries, reserving a handful for topping.

Transfer the batter to the prepared pan and bake for 45 to 55 minutes, until a toothpick comes out clean. Remove the pan from the oven and let the cake cool completely before trying to remove the cake from the pan. Flip the Bundt pan over onto a serving dish to remove the cake.

To make the glaze, in a microwave-safe bowl, melt together the chocolate and coconut oil on 50 percent power in 15-second increments, stirring in between, until smooth. Drizzle the glaze over the cake. Decorate the cake with the reserved raspberries just before serving.

Triple Chocolate Cupcakes

Chocolate on top and chocolate inside . . . a truly chocolate cupcake! The only requirement here is that you must absolutely love chocolate, because these cupcakes have three times the chocolatey goodness.

Makes 12 cupcakes

CUPCAKES

1 cup (120 g) all-purpose flour

½ cup (40 g) unsweetened cocoa powder

⅓ cup (68 g) granulated sugar

1 tsp baking soda

¼ tsp salt

½ cup (90 g) vegan chocolate chips

¾ cup (180 ml) almond milk

⅓ cup (75 g) packed brown sugar

2 tbsp (37 g) pumpkin puree

¼ cup (60 g) coconut oil, melted

1 tbsp (15 ml) distilled white vinegar

2 tsp (10 ml) vanilla extract

WHIPPED GANACHE FROSTING

2 cups (360 g) chopped vegan chocolate

1 cup (240 ml) full-fat coconut milk (see Note)

Vegan chocolate shavings, for topping

Preheat the oven to 350°F (180°C, or gas mark 4) and line a muffin tin with 12 cupcake liners.

To make the cupcakes, in a large bowl, stir together the flour, cocoa powder, granulated sugar, baking soda, salt and chocolate chips until combined.

In a medium bowl, whisk together the almond milk, brown sugar, pumpkin puree, coconut oil, vinegar and vanilla until smooth. Pour the wet ingredients over the dry and stir with a rubber spatula until a batter forms and no dry spots remain.

Use a cookie scooper to fill the liners about three-fourths of the way full. Bake the cupcakes for 20 to 22 minutes, until a toothpick inserted into the center comes out clean. Remove the pan from the oven and let the cupcakes cool for 40 minutes.

To make the frosting, place the chopped chocolate in a heatproof bowl and set aside. Pour the coconut milk into a small pot and set over medium heat. Bring the milk to a boil and then remove it from the heat. Pour the milk over the chocolate and let it sit for 4 minutes. After 4 minutes, whisk the mixture until a smooth chocolate forms. Cover the bowl with plastic wrap and chill in the refrigerator for 30 to 40 minutes.

Remove the chocolate ganache from the refrigerator; it should be very thick—that's exactly how you want it. Use an electric mixer to beat the chocolate until it's light and fluffy, 1 to 2 minutes. Place the whipped ganache into a piping bag and decorate the cupcakes. Top the cupcakes with chocolate shavings. Store them in the refrigerator.

Note: Any brand of coconut milk will work, but I prefer the Thai Kitchen brand.

No-Bake Cookies and Cream Cheesecake

One of my favorite vegan cheesecake recipes is just a simple no-bake cream cheese and yogurt mix. I always forget how delicious it is and whenever I make it, I wonder why I don't make it more often!

Serves 10

CRUST

18 chocolate sandwich cookies (gluten free if necessary)

3 tbsp (42 g) vegan butter, melted

FILLING

1 (8-oz [227-g]) package vegan cream cheese, at room temperature

¾ cup (180 g) plain vegan yogurt

⅔ cup (80 g) confectioners' sugar, sifted

Line an 8 x 4–inch (20 x 10–cm) pan with parchment paper, leaving some overhang so you can easily remove the cheesecake.

To make the crust, place the cookies in a food processor and pulse until fine crumbs form. Add the melted butter and pulse until combined. Press two-thirds of the mixture into the bottom of the prepared pan and tamp it down evenly.

To make the filling, in a large bowl with an electric mixer, beat the cream cheese until smooth and creamy. Add the yogurt and confectioners' sugar and beat until combined. Pour the filling over the crust. Top with the remaining cookie crumbles. Cover the pan with plastic wrap and chill for at least 12 hours or overnight. Keep the cheesecake chilled until ready to serve and then cut it into 10 slices.

Double Chocolate Cream Pie 🅖🅕

Chocolate crust, silky chocolate filling and chocolate whipped cream conspire to make it pretty hard to stop eating this double chocolate cream pie. Your inner chocolate lover is going to freak out upon your first forkful of this scrumptious pie.

Serves 10

CRUST

½ cup (60 g) all-purpose flour or gluten-free baking flour

½ cup (60 g) almond flour

2 tbsp (18 g) tapioca flour

¼ cup (20 g) Dutch-processed cocoa powder

1 tbsp (15 ml) maple syrup

5 tbsp (75 g) cold vegan butter, cubed

FILLING

1 (16-oz [454-g]) package silken tofu

⅓ cup (68 g) granulated sugar

2 tbsp (10 g) Dutch-processed cocoa powder

2 tsp (10 ml) vanilla extract

1 cup (180 g) vegan dark chocolate chips, melted

TOPPING

Whipped coconut cream

Vegan chocolate shavings

Preheat the oven to 350°F (180°C, or gas mark 4). Coat a 9-inch (23-cm) tart pan with nonstick spray.

To make the crust, place the flours and cocoa powder in a food processor and pulse to combine. Add the maple syrup and butter and pulse until a dough ball begins to form. Press the dough into the bottom and firmly up the sides of the pan. Bake the crust for 7 to 8 minutes, or until golden brown. Remove the pan from the oven and let the crust cool completely, 20 to 30 minutes.

To make the filling, place the tofu, sugar, cocoa powder and vanilla in a food processor and blend until smooth, about 1 minute. Add the melted chocolate and continue blending until well combined, about 30 seconds. Scrape the filling into the crust and use a spatula to smooth the top evenly. Cover with plastic wrap and chill for 6 hours or overnight.

For the topping, remove the chilled pie from the refrigerator and spread whipped coconut cream over the top, smoothing it with a spatula. Sprinkle with the chocolate shavings.

Chocolate Hazelnut Tart gf

A dessert with chocolate and hazelnut makes me so giddy that I've considered changing my blog name to Hazelnut Plus Chocolate. This tart is high up on my list of the best desserts in this book. What I love most about it is its hazelnut shortbread crust and smooth chocolate filling, a perfect combination that you won't be able to get enough of.

Serves 16

CRUST

2 cups (240 g) hazelnut flour

½ cup (72 g) tapioca flour

¼ cup (60 g) coconut oil, melted

3 tbsp (45 ml) maple syrup

¼ tsp sea salt

FILLING

2 cups (360 g) chopped vegan chocolate

1 cup (240 ml) coconut milk

⅓ cup (100 g) vegan chocolate hazelnut spread

TOPPING

Chopped hazelnuts

Vegan chocolate shavings

Preheat the oven to 350°F (180°C, or gas mark 4) and coat a 14 x 4½-inch (36 x 11.5–cm) tart pan with nonstick spray.

To make the crust, in a bowl, stir together the flours, coconut oil, maple syrup and salt until well combined. Press the dough tightly and evenly into the bottom and up the sides of the tart pan. Bake the crust for 10 to 12 minutes, or until it's golden brown. Remove the pan from the oven and let it cool completely, 20 to 30 minutes.

To make the filling, place the chopped chocolate in a heatproof bowl and set aside. Add the coconut milk to a saucepan or small pot and bring it to a boil over medium-high heat. Remove the milk from the heat, and then pour it over the chocolate and let it sit for 4 minutes before stirring until smooth. Add the chocolate hazelnut spread and stir until well combined. Pour the filling into the tart and spread it evenly to the corners using a spatula. Cover with plastic wrap and chill for at least 2 hours.

For the topping, remove the chilled pie from the refrigerator and sprinkle with the hazelnuts and chocolate shavings.

Molten Lava Cakes for Two

The classic molten lava cake has a reputation for being one of the most decadent desserts of all time—it's certainly in the Chocolate Hall of Fame for its contributions to chocolate lovers everywhere. This vegan version definitely isn't lacking in taste or texture. Just like the traditional version, you will love digging into the warm, chocolatey center.

Serves 2

½ cup (90 g) vegan dark chocolate chips

2 tbsp (28 g) vegan butter

¼ cup (60 g) unsweetened applesauce

2 tbsp (30 ml) almond milk

1 tsp vanilla extract

¾ tsp distilled white vinegar

5 tbsp (40 g) all-purpose flour

2 tbsp (10 g) unsweetened cocoa powder, plus more for dusting

¼ tsp baking soda

⅛ tsp salt

Preheat the oven to 425°F (220°C, or gas mark 7) and coat two 4½-ounce (125-g) ramekins with nonstick spray or vegan shortening.

In a microwave-safe bowl, melt together the dark chocolate chips and vegan butter on 50 percent power in 15-second increments, stirring in between, until smooth. Whisk in the applesauce, almond milk, vanilla and vinegar until incorporated. Sift the flour, cocoa powder, baking soda and salt on top and stir until combined.

Transfer the batter to the prepared ramekins. Place the ramekins on a baking sheet and bake for 12 to 13 minutes. The tops should be crusted but the center still jiggly. Remove the ramekins from the oven and flip them out onto serving plates. Dust with cocoa powder if desired and serve.

Maraschino Cherry Cupcakes

I love nothing more than a cupcake piled high with frosting, and I promise these cupcakes taste as good as they look! Super rich and unbelievably moist chocolate cake is topped with sweet cherry buttercream and maraschino cherries. Think chocolate-covered cherries but in cake form.

Makes 9 cupcakes

CUPCAKES

1 cup (120 g) all-purpose flour

½ cup (40 g) unsweetened cocoa powder

1 tsp baking soda

¼ tsp salt

¼ cup (60 g) coconut oil, melted

⅓ cup (68 g) granulated sugar

⅓ cup (75 g) packed brown sugar

2 tsp (10 ml) vanilla extract

2 tbsp (30 g) unsweetened applesauce

¾ cup (180 ml) almond milk

1 tbsp (15 ml) distilled white vinegar

¼ cup (36 g) maraschino cherries, stems removed

FROSTING

½ cup (113 g) vegan butter, at room temperature

3 tbsp (42 g) vegan shortening

½ tsp vanilla extract

2½ to 3 cups (290 to 345 g) confectioners' sugar

1 tbsp (15 ml) maraschino juice (from the jar)

9 maraschino cherries, to top

Preheat the oven to 350°F (180°C, or gas mark 4) and prepare a cupcake tin with 9 liners.

To make the cupcakes, in a medium bowl, stir together the flour, cocoa powder, baking soda and salt. In a large bowl using an electric mixer, beat together the coconut oil, granulated sugar, brown sugar and vanilla until creamy, about 1 minute. Add the applesauce, almond milk and vinegar and mix until combined. Fold in the flour mixture, then fold in the cherries.

Use a cookie scooper or an ice cream scoop to fill the liners two-thirds of the way with batter. Bake the cupcakes for 20 to 22 minutes, until a toothpick inserted into the center comes out clean. Remove the pan from the oven and let the cupcakes cool completely.

To make the frosting, in a large bowl using an electric mixer, beat the butter until creamy, about 1 minute. Add the shortening and vanilla and beat until smooth. Sift the confectioners' sugar on top and beat until smooth, about 1 minute. Add the cherry juice and mix just until combined. Transfer the frosting to a piping bag and frost the cupcakes. Top each cupcake with a cherry just before serving.

Note: For a more vibrant pink frosting, add 1 to 2 drops of natural red food coloring.

Chocolate Tiramisu Sheet Cake

With four amazing layers, this concoction is a chocolate spin on the classic Italian dessert. This one is a bit time-consuming, but worth it if you are baking to impress a big crowd. Or it's easy to cut this recipe in half and to bake it in an 8 x 8–inch (20 x 20–cm) pan for a smaller group.

Serves 18

CHOCOLATE CAKE LAYER

2 cups (240 g) all-purpose flour

⅔ cup (55 g) Dutch-processed cocoa powder

2 tsp (6 g) baking soda

½ tsp sea salt

½ cup (90 g) vegan chocolate chips

½ cup (120 g) coconut oil, melted

⅔ cup (148 g) packed brown sugar

⅔ cup (135 g) granulated sugar

1½ cups (360 ml) almond milk, at room temperature

¼ cup (60 g) unsweetened apple-sauce, at room temperature

2 tsp (10 ml) vanilla extract

2 tbsp (30 ml) distilled white vinegar

⅓ cup (80 ml) hot water

1 tbsp (6 g) espresso powder

CHOCOLATE FILLING LAYER

1 cup (227 g) silken tofu, drained

¼ cup (60 ml) almond milk

¼ cup (64 g) cashew butter

¾ cup (135 g) vegan chocolate chips, melted

CREAM LAYER

1 (14-oz [414-ml]) can coconut cream, chilled

1 (8-oz [227-g]) container vegan cream cheese (almond milk based)

3 tbsp (24 g) confectioners' sugar

1 tsp vanilla bean paste or extract

TOPPING

1 (8-oz [227-g]) container coconut whipped topping

Dutch-processed cocoa powder, for dusting

Preheat the oven to 350°F (180°C, or gas mark 4). Coat a 9 x 13–inch (23 x 33–cm) baking pan with nonstick spray and line the bottom with parchment paper.

To make the cake, in a medium bowl, stir together the flour, cocoa powder, baking soda, salt and chocolate chips until combined. In a large bowl using an electric mixer, beat together the coconut oil, brown sugar and granulated sugar until combined, about 30 seconds. Add the almond milk, applesauce and vanilla and beat until combined. Stir in the vinegar. Add the dry ingredients to the wet and mix until a batter forms.

Transfer the batter to the prepared pan and bake for 20 to 24 minutes, until a toothpick inserted into the center comes out clean. Remove the pan from the oven and let the cake cool completely. Use a toothpick to poke several holes in the top of the cake. Stir together the water and espresso powder and brush the mixture over the cake.

To make the filling, place the tofu, almond milk and cashew butter in a blender and blend until smooth. Add the melted chocolate and continue blending until incorporated. Pour the mixture over the cake and use a rubber spatula to spread it in an even layer. Cover the pan with plastic wrap and chill in the refrigerator for 30 minutes.

To make the cream, open the can of coconut cream and scrape off the cream from the top. Set the cream aside. In a medium bowl using an electric mixer, beat the cream cheese until soft and creamy, about 30 seconds. Add the reserved coconut cream and beat until well combined. Add the confectioners' sugar and vanilla bean paste and beat until incorporated. Spread the cream over the chocolate filling in an even layer.

For the topping, pipe or spoon dollops of cream over the top of the cake. Dust with cocoa powder. Keep the cake refrigerated when not being served.

Pretzel-Crusted Chocolate Strawberry Tart

This past Thanksgiving I had the best idea I've ever had—a pumpkin pie crusted with pretzels. Since then, I haven't been able to stop thinking about it. It was amazing! The pretzel crust was so good that it crept into my concept of what a chocolate strawberry tart could be. Also, you can easily swap out regular pretzels for gluten free and you will never taste the difference!

Serves 10

CRUST

5 cups (290 g) mini pretzels (gluten free if necessary)

¼ cup (50 g) granulated sugar

10 tbsp (140 g) vegan butter, melted

FILLING

1 cup (240 ml) coconut cream or full-fat coconut milk

6 oz (168 g) vegan dark chocolate, chopped

2 tbsp (30 g) natural almond butter

2 tsp (10 ml) vanilla extract

⅛ tsp salt

TOPPING

1 lb (454 g) fresh strawberries, stems removed and thinly sliced

Preheat the oven to 350°F (180°C, or gas mark 4). Coat a 9-inch (23-cm) tart pan with nonstick spray.

To make the crust, place the pretzels in a food processor and pulse until small crumbles form, about 10 seconds. Add the sugar and butter and pulse until the mixture resembles wet sand, 15 to 20 seconds. Press the mixture evenly into the bottom and up the sides of the prepared tart pan. Use the bottom of a glass to pack it tightly. Place the tart pan on a baking sheet and bake the crust for 6 to 8 minutes, until golden brown. Watch it carefully to make sure it doesn't burn. Remove it from the oven and let it cool completely.

To make the filling, place the coconut cream, chocolate, almond butter, vanilla and salt in a food processor or blender and blend until smooth, about 10 seconds. Pour the filling into the crust. Cover the pan with plastic wrap and chill in the refrigerator for 1 hour.

For the topping, when ready to serve, remove the tart from the refrigerator and decorate the top with the strawberries.

Triple Chocolate Hand Pies 🅖🄵

For when you are feeling particularly nostalgic, these Triple Chocolate Hand Pies will always be there for you. This American classic comes to you reimagined with plenty of chocolate—and may spark new family traditions. If anything can, it's a chocolate crust wrapped around a sweet chocolate filling and then topped with chocolate glaze!

Makes 5 hand pies

CRUST

1¼ cups (150 g) all-purpose flour or gluten-free baking flour

¼ cup (36 g) tapioca flour

2 tbsp (10 g) unsweetened cocoa powder

1 tbsp (15 ml) maple syrup

½ cup (113 g) cold vegan butter, cubed

3 to 4 tbsp (45 to 60 ml) cold water

Almond milk, for brushing

FILLING

¾ cup (135 g) vegan chocolate chips

2 tbsp (28 g) vegan butter

2 tbsp (30 ml) almond milk

TOPPING

⅓ cup (60 g) vegan chocolate chips

1 tsp coconut oil

Crushed Oreos

Preheat the oven to 350°F (180°C, or gas mark 4) and line a baking sheet with parchment paper.

To make the crust, place the all-purpose flour, tapioca flour and cocoa powder in a food processor and pulse to combine. Add the maple syrup and butter and pulse for 5 to 10 seconds, until small crumbs form. Add the water, 1 tablespoon (15 ml) at a time, and pulse until a dough ball forms.

Place the dough between two pieces of parchment paper and roll it into a 10 x 6–inch (25 x 15–cm) rectangle about ⅛ inch (3 mm) thick. Neaten the edges and use a knife to cut ten 2 x 3–inch (5 x 7.5–cm) rectangles. Place the rectangles on the prepared baking sheet. Use a fork to poke air holes in 5 of the rectangles.

To make the filling, in a microwave-safe bowl, melt together the chocolate chips and butter on 50 percent power in 10-second increments, stirring in between, until smooth. Whisk in the almond milk. Spread the filling in the center of the 5 rectangles without holes, leaving room around the edges, and then top with the second rectangle crust (the one with the holes). Use a fork to crimp the edges together. Brush the crust with almond milk.

Bake the hand pies for 15 to 20 minutes, until the edges begin to crisp and the center puffs slightly.

To make the topping, in a microwave-safe bowl, melt together the chocolate chips and coconut oil on 50 percent power in 10-second increments, stirring in between, until smooth. Brush the chocolate mixture over the slightly cooled hand pies and sprinkle with the crushed Oreos while the glaze is still wet.

Double Chocolate Crepe Cake

Crepe cakes are just breathtaking, aren't they? So many layers and yet you never have to turn on the oven. This cake is so easy to make and sure to wow!

Serves 10

FILLING

2 (14-oz [414-ml]) cans coconut cream, chilled

3 tbsp (24 g) confectioners' sugar, sifted

CREPES

2½ cups (300 g) all-purpose flour

½ cup (40 g) Dutch-processed cocoa powder

1 tbsp (9 g) tapioca flour

½ tsp salt

¼ cup (60 ml) maple syrup

2 tsp (10 ml) vanilla extract

2½ cups (600 ml) almond milk

Vegan chocolate shavings, for topping

To make the filling, chill a glass bowl in the refrigerator for 15 minutes prior to beginning.

Remove the cans of coconut cream from the refrigerator, open the cans, scrape all the cream from the tops of the cans, leaving the coconut water (you can save this for future recipes), and place it in the chilled bowl. With an electric mixer, beat the coconut cream until creamy and fluffy, about 3 minutes. Add the confectioners' sugar and beat until combined. Place the whipped cream in an airtight container and chill until ready to use. It will firm up more once chilled.

To make the crepes, place the flour, cocoa powder, tapioca flour, salt, maple syrup, vanilla and almond milk in a food processor or blender and blend until smooth. Let the batter rest for 15 minutes.

Coat a large nonstick pan with nonstick spray and place it over low heat. Tip: Low heat is very important here. Once the pan is heated, hold it just above the heat and add ¼ cup (60 ml) of the batter to the center of the pan. Immediately swirl the pan in a circular motion so the batter spreads out into a thin layer and evenly coats the pan. Cook the crepe for 1 to 2 minutes. The edges should start to pull away when it's ready. Gently loosen the crepe with a spatula and flip. Cook for 1 minute on the other side. Slide the crepe out of the pan onto a plate and repeat the process until you have used all the batter. Let your crepes cool completely before assembling the cake.

To assemble the cake, place one crepe on a serving dish and spread a thin layer of whipped cream over it. Top with another crepe and repeat until you have used all the crepes. Top with a layer of whipped cream and sprinkle with the chocolate shavings. Chill in the refrigerator until ready to serve.

Note: For a more aesthetically pleasing presentation, flip a bowl upside down on top of each crepe and use a knife to make them all the same size before assembling the cake.

Secret Chocolate Zucchini Bread

Here, chocolate bread is secretly infused with zucchini to help keep this loaf moist while remaining rich, chocolatey and decadent. This chocolate zucchini bread is a great way to add more vegetables to your diet, not to mention a perfect excuse to eat cake for dinner!

Serves 12

ZUCCHINI BREAD

1 tbsp (7 g) flax meal

2 tbsp (30 ml) water

½ cup (120 g) coconut oil, melted

¾ cup (165 g) packed brown sugar

¾ cup (180 ml) almond milk, at room temperature

1 tbsp (15 ml) distilled white vinegar

1 tsp vanilla extract

2 medium zucchini, peeled and grated

2¼ cups (270 g) all-purpose flour

½ cup (40 g) unsweetened cocoa powder

1 tbsp (9 g) tapioca flour

1 tsp baking soda

½ tsp baking powder

¼ tsp salt

TOPPING

½ cup (90 g) vegan chocolate chips

½ tsp coconut oil

Handful of vegan chocolate curls

Preheat the oven to 350°F (180°C, or gas mark 4). Coat a 9 x 5–inch (23 x 13–cm) loaf pan with nonstick spray and line it with parchment paper so you can easily remove the loaf.

To make the bread, in a small bowl, stir together the flax meal and water and set it aside to gel, about 5 minutes.

Meanwhile, in a large bowl, stir together the coconut oil, brown sugar, almond milk, vinegar and vanilla until well combined and creamy. Place the grated zucchini between two paper towels and squeeze out the excess liquid, then add the zucchini and flax mixture to the wet ingredients and stir until well combined.

In a medium bowl, stir together the flour, cocoa powder, tapioca flour, baking soda, baking powder and salt and then gradually add the mixture to the wet ingredients, stirring just until combined and no dry spots remain; try not to overmix.

Transfer the mixture to the prepared pan and bake for 60 to 65 minutes, until a toothpick inserted into the center of the loaf comes out clean. Remove the pan from the oven and let cool. Turn out the loaf from the pan and peel off the parchment paper.

To make the topping, in a microwave-safe bowl, melt together the chocolate and coconut oil on 50 percent power for 1 to 2 minutes, or until melted. Stir to combine. Drizzle the chocolate over the loaf, decorate with the chocolate curls and cut into slices to serve.

Candies
and other goodies

My goal for this chapter was lofty, to say the least: a set of chocolate treats that you absolutely can't live without! After many late nights of recipe testing, I'm happy to report that I do feel that way, so of course I hope you will too. From Chocolate-Dipped Churros on page 80 (seriously the best!) to Peanut Butter Chocolate Cups (page 88), I've covered it all. If you are looking for something random, something delicious or something out of this world—good! Pick a recipe and get started on one of your new favorite chocolate treats.

Chocolate-Dipped Churros

If you are afraid to make churros at home, then this recipe is perfect for you. The dough is so easy to make—pop the churros in some frying oil and they are done within a minute. Roll them in cinnamon sugar and you will be dipping them in chocolate in no time!

Serves 20 to 25

DOUGH

1½ cups (180 g) all-purpose flour

1 tsp ground cinnamon

1½ cups (360 ml) water

5 tbsp (75 g) vegan butter

3 tbsp (36 g) granulated sugar

½ tsp salt

Vegetable oil, for frying

COATING

½ cup (100 g) granulated sugar

1 tsp ground cinnamon

DIP

½ cup (90 g) vegan dark chocolate chips

1 tsp coconut oil

To make the dough, in a mixing bowl, stir together the flour and cinnamon. Place the water, butter, sugar and salt in a nonstick frying pan and set over medium-low heat. Whisk until smooth. Bring the mixture to a boil and then remove the pan from the heat. Immediately add the flour mixture and whisk until it starts to thicken. Change to a silicone spatula and continue stirring until a dough forms. Let the dough cool for 5 to 10 minutes or until it's cool enough to handle.

Transfer the dough to a pastry bag fitted with the star attachment and line a baking sheet with paper towels.

To make the coating, in a bowl, mix together the sugar and cinnamon and set aside.

Fill a pot or cast-iron skillet with 1 to 2 inches (2.5 to 5 cm) of oil and set it over medium heat. Once the oil reaches 370°F (188°C) on a deep-fry thermometer, decrease the heat to medium-low. Carefully pipe a 4- to 5-inch (10- to 13-cm) churro directly into the oil and use a knife or kitchen shears to snip off the dough. Cook the churro until golden brown, 30 to 40 seconds. You can add up to three churros in one batch, just be careful not to let them touch.

Remove the churros from the oil using tongs and place them on the prepared baking sheet. Let them cool for about 1 minute before tossing them in the sugar-cinnamon mixture. Repeat the process until you have used all the dough.

To make the dip, in a microwave-safe bowl, melt together the chocolate and coconut oil on 50 percent power in 15-second increments, stirring in between, until smooth. Dip each churro in the chocolate and serve.

No-Churn Rocky Road Ice Cream gf

Making ice cream doesn't have to be labor-intensive. This recipe is simple to make and it's not just delicious—it can also be customized to your taste. If you don't like walnuts, how about almonds? Hazelnuts? Pecans? Or even chopped peanuts?

Serves 20

1 (11.6-oz [330-g]) can sweetened condensed coconut milk

½ cup (120 g) vegan yogurt

½ cup (40 g) Dutch-processed cocoa powder

2 tsp (10 ml) vanilla extract

¼ tsp sea salt

2 (14-oz [414-ml]) cans coconut cream, chilled

¼ cup (45 g) vegan chocolate chips

1 tsp coconut oil

¼ cup (6 g) mini vegan marshmallows, chopped (gluten free if necessary)

¼ cup (25 g) walnuts or nut of choice, chopped

Place a 9 x 5–inch (23 x 13–cm) baking pan in the freezer to chill.

In a mixing bowl, stir together the condensed coconut milk, yogurt, cocoa powder, vanilla and salt until smooth. In a large bowl using an electric mixer, beat the coconut cream for 2 to 3 minutes. It should become lighter and fluffier. Add the yogurt mixture and stir until combined and no streaks remain.

In a small, microwave-safe bowl, melt together the chocolate and coconut oil on 50 percent power in 15-second increments, stirring in between, until smooth.

Remove the pan from the freezer and scoop about ½ cup (120 g) of the coconut mixture into the pan. Drizzle the chocolate over the top and sprinkle on some marshmallows and walnuts. Repeat this process until you have filled the pan and used all of the ingredients. Cover the pan with plastic wrap and freeze overnight.

Dark Chocolate Almond Bark ⓖⓕ

Chocolate bark is a classic dessert, and my favorite thing about making it is the endless combinations and possibilities. For me, I like it simple with chopped almonds, pretzel pieces and flaky sea salt, but I encourage you to get creative and add your favorite nuts or dried fruit.

Serves 15

12 oz (336 g) vegan chocolate, chopped

3 cups (414 g) dry-roasted almonds

¼ cup (10 g) mini pretzels (gluten free if necessary)

Flaky sea salt

Line a baking sheet with parchment paper.

Place the chocolate in a heat-proof bowl and place the bowl over a small pot of simmering water. Stir the chocolate frequently until smooth. Add the almonds and stir until they are all well coated. Transfer the chocolate to the baking sheet and spread it out in an even layer. Top with the pretzel pieces.

Let the chocolate set at room temperature for 2 hours before breaking it into pieces (or you can chill the chocolate until it is solid). Break the chocolate into pieces and sprinkle with sea salt.

Salted Caramel Chocolate Truffles

Date caramel is my favorite kind of vegan caramel. It takes only a few minutes to whip up, dip in chocolate and top with flaky sea salt. A simple little treat. I like to keep these in my freezer and then defrost a few at a time for about 15 minutes before devouring them.

Makes 12 pieces

CARAMEL

2 cups (360 g) soft Medjool dates, pitted and chopped

3 tbsp (50 g) natural peanut butter

1 tbsp (14 g) coconut oil, melted

⅛ tsp sea salt

CHOCOLATE COATING

1 cup (180 g) vegan chocolate chips

2 tsp (10 g) coconut oil

Flaky sea salt

Line an 8 x 4–inch (20 x 10–cm) loaf pan with parchment paper, leaving some overhang so you can easily remove it, and then chill in the freezer for 15 minutes.

To make the caramel, place the chopped dates, peanut butter, coconut oil and salt in a food processor or high-speed blender and blend on high for 1 minute. Stop and scrape the sides and then continue to blend until smooth, about 1 minute. Press the mixture into the bottom of the prepared pan. Return the pan to the freezer.

To make the coating, in a microwave-safe bowl, melt together the chocolate chips and coconut oil on 50 percent power for 1 minute. Stir until the chocolate is smooth.

Remove the pan from the freezer and use the parchment-paper handles to remove the caramel from the pan. Cut it into 12 evenly sized pieces. Use a fork to dip each caramel into the chocolate, let the excess chocolate drip back into the bowl and then place it on a piece of parchment paper to harden. Repeat until you have covered all the caramels. Return the caramels to the freezer until the chocolate is solid, about 5 minutes. Sprinkle with the flaky sea salt.

Peanut Butter Chocolate Cups gf

I love this combination so much I named my business after it! This simple yet delicious recipe lives up to the glorious combination of peanut butter and chocolate. While my love for this combo is undying, you can make it your own and sub in any nut butter.

Makes 12 pieces

1 cup (180 g) vegan chocolate chips

⅓ cup (85 g) natural peanut butter

1 tbsp (15 ml) maple syrup

Sesame seeds, for topping

Prepare a baking sheet with 12 mini cupcake liners and then set it aside.

In a double boiler or microwave-safe bowl, melt the chocolate chips on 50 percent power in 15-second increments, stirring in between, until smooth.

Spoon half of the chocolate into each liner. Smooth the chocolate to cover the bottom and halfway up the sides. Place the baking sheet in the freezer while you prepare the peanut butter.

In a bowl, stir together the peanut butter and maple syrup until combined. Spoon the mixture into the bottom of each chocolate-lined cupcake liner and then top with the remaining chocolate. Sprinkle with the sesame seeds. Return the candies to the freezer until the chocolate is solid, 10 to 15 minutes.

Turtle Candy Clusters gf

Pecan lovers, this is for you! Toasted pecans are just delicious, aren't they? Especially with chocolate and a touch of salt. For a quick treat, I like to keep these in my freezer and eat them without thawing—because they will never fully freeze.

Makes 15 pieces

60 pecans halves, lightly toasted

1 (11.6-oz [330-g]) can sweetened condensed coconut milk

1 cup (200 g) coconut sugar

5 tbsp (75 g) vegan butter

¼ cup (36 g) tapioca flour

1 tsp vanilla extract

1 cup (180 g) vegan dark chocolate chips

½ tsp coconut oil

Flaky sea salt

Line two baking sheets with parchment paper, arrange the pecans in clusters of 4 on the parchment paper and then set the baking sheet aside.

In a pot over medium-low heat, combine the condensed coconut milk, coconut sugar, butter, tapioca flour and vanilla and cook, stirring, until smooth. Bring the mixture to a boil, lower the heat to a simmer and cook for 10 to 15 minutes, until thickened. Remove the pot from the heat and let the mixture cool for about 15 minutes. Spoon about ½ tablespoon (8 ml) of caramel over each pecan cluster, let them harden slightly at room temperature for about 10 minutes and then add another layer of caramel sauce.

In a microwave-safe bowl, melt together the dark chocolate chips and coconut oil on 50 percent power in 15-second increments, stirring in between, until smooth. Spoon the chocolate over each cluster. Sprinkle with sea salt. Chill the clusters in the freezer until ready to serve.

Chocolate Crunch Bars

Don't let the size fool you—there is quite a combination of health and luscious chocolate packed into each of these crunch bars. These treats make a perfect snack, dessert or quick, indulgent pick-me-up all while using simple and natural ingredients.

Makes 10 bars

3 cups (93 g) rice cereal (gluten free if necessary)

1 tbsp (10 g) chia seeds

⅓ cup (85 g) natural peanut butter

7 tbsp (105 ml) maple syrup

3 tbsp (45 g) coconut oil

1 tsp vanilla extract

CHOCOLATE COATING

1 cup (180 g) vegan chocolate chips

2 tsp (10 g) coconut oil

Culinary-grade rose petals, crumbled, for topping

Line an 8 x 8–inch (20 x 20–cm) pan with parchment paper, leaving some overhang so you can easily remove the bars.

Place the cereal and chia seeds in a large mixing bowl and set aside.

In a microwave-safe bowl, gently melt together the peanut butter, maple syrup, coconut oil and vanilla on 50 percent power for about 15 seconds, and then stir until smooth. Pour the mixture into the bowl with the cereal and use a large wooden spoon or rubber spatula to stir until all of the cereal is well coated. Press the mixture into the bottom of the pan and pack it down tightly. Place the pan in the refrigerator and chill for 30 minutes.

Remove the pan from the refrigerator, use the parchment-paper handles to remove the block of bars from the pan and cut them into 10 evenly sized bars. Place them in the freezer while you melt the chocolate.

To make the coating, in a microwave-safe bowl, melt together the chocolate and coconut oil on 50 percent power in 15-second increments, stirring in between, until smooth. Cover the rice bars in the chocolate and chill in the freezer until solid, 10 to 15 minutes. Sprinkle with the rose petals before serving.

Toasted Coconut Chocolate Caramel Bars

These crunchy chocolate peanut butter coconut candy bars have a really nice, nuanced flavor because of the date caramel. I love them cold, although they are great at room temperature, too!

Makes 6 bars

COCONUT CARAMEL LAYER

14 Medjool dates, pitted

¼ cup (60 ml) maple syrup

2 tbsp (32 g) natural peanut butter

2 tbsp (10 g) Dutch-processed cocoa powder

1 tsp vanilla extract

⅛ tsp salt

¼ cup (60 ml) water

3 cups (180 g) toasted coconut chips, plus more for topping

PEANUT BUTTER LAYER

6 tbsp (96 g) natural peanut butter

¼ cup (36 g) dry-roasted peanuts

CHOCOLATE COATING

1½ cups (270 g) vegan chocolate chips, plus more for topping

1 tbsp (14 g) coconut oil

Line a 9 x 5–inch (23 x 13–cm) loaf pan with parchment paper, leaving some overhang so you can easily remove the bars.

To make the coconut caramel layer, place the dates, maple syrup, peanut butter, cocoa powder, vanilla and salt in a food processor and blend until incorporated, 20 to 30 seconds. Slowly add the water and continue to blend until smooth, then blend for an additional 30 seconds.

Place the coconut chips in a large mixing bowl, add the date mixture (it will be very sticky) and use a large spoon or rubber spatula to fold the mixture together until all the coconut chips are coated.

Press the mixture evenly into the bottom of the prepared pan and pack it down tightly. Transfer the pan to the freezer and chill for 20 minutes. Remove the pan from the freezer, use the parchment-paper handles to remove the block of bars from the pan and cut the block into 6 evenly sized bars.

For the peanut butter layer, spread a layer of peanut butter over each bar, sprinkle with the peanuts and then return the bars to the freezer for 10 minutes.

To make the coating, in a microwave-safe bowl, melt together the chocolate chips and coconut oil on 50 percent power in 15-second increments, stirring in between, until smooth. Coat each bar in chocolate, sprinkle with additional coconut chips and freeze until the chocolate is solid, 10 to 15 minutes. Store the bars in an airtight container in the refrigerator.

Cold Brew Chocolate Popsicles

Chocolate and coffee are a perfect pair, and here they work together to bring you the most delicious summer treat!

Makes 6 popsicles

½ cup (120 g) vanilla-flavored vegan yogurt

½ cup (120 ml) full-fat coconut milk

1 cup (240 ml) cold brew coffee

1 tsp vanilla extract

½ cup (90 g) vegan chocolate chips, divided

1 tsp coconut oil

In a medium bowl, whisk together the yogurt and coconut milk until smooth. Add the coffee and vanilla and stir to combine. Divide the mixture among 6 popsicle molds and distribute ¼ cup (45 g) of the chocolate chips among the molds. Insert popsicle sticks and freeze the popsicles for at least 6 hours (or overnight).

In a microwave-safe bowl, melt together the remaining ¼ cup (45 g) of chocolate chips and the coconut oil on 50 percent power in 15-second increments, stirring in between, until smooth.

To remove the popsicles, run the molds under warm water for 1 minute or until the popsicles slide out. Drizzle the melted chocolate over the popsicles and serve.

Note: You can refreeze these after applying the drizzle to get a crusty chocolate coating!

Snack attack

Turn to this chapter for when it's all about the quick and easy. Just because you're on the go is no excuse not to have chocolate in your life! The bars, bites and other snackables collected here are meant for simple and rapid prep, recipes that you can go to when it's too hot to turn on the oven or when you need a quick pick-me-up after the gym. Save them in the fridge, or take them with you—like No-Bake Chocolate Oat Bars (page 100). Added bonus: Every recipe in this chapter can be made gluten free—with extra chocolate love, of course.

No-Bake Chocolate Oat Bars gf

Snacks are a must in my house—especially chocolate ones. These no-bake bars are very easy to whip up, require no bake time and keep fresh in the refrigerator for a couple of weeks . . . if they last that long.

Makes 16 bars

¾ cup (135 g) vegan chocolate chips

¼ cup (56 g) vegan butter

¼ cup (60 ml) maple syrup

½ cup (136 g) almond butter

1½ cups (135 g) rolled oats (gluten free if necessary)

⅓ cup (30 g) unsweetened coconut flakes

Line an 8 x 8–inch (20 x 20–cm) pan with parchment paper, leaving some overhang so you can easily remove the bars.

In a microwave-safe bowl, melt together the chocolate chips and butter on 50 percent power for 30 to 40 seconds, stir, cook for 15 to 20 seconds longer and then stir until smooth. Stir in the maple syrup and almond butter.

In a mixing bowl, stir together the oats and coconut flakes, and then add the chocolate mixture and stir until everything is evenly coated in chocolate. Press the mixture into the bottom of the prepared pan, cover with plastic wrap and chill in the refrigerator for 20 minutes or until ready to serve.

Using the parchment-paper handles, remove the bars from the pan and cut into 16 evenly sized squares.

Blueberry Chocolate Energy Bites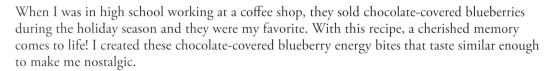

When I was in high school working at a coffee shop, they sold chocolate-covered blueberries during the holiday season and they were my favorite. With this recipe, a cherished memory comes to life! I created these chocolate-covered blueberry energy bites that taste similar enough to make me nostalgic.

Makes 14 bites

10 Medjool dates, pitted

1 cup (146 g) raw cashews

⅛ tsp salt

¾ cup (120 g) dried blueberries

3 oz (84 g) vegan chocolate, chopped

½ tsp coconut oil

Line a baking sheet with parchment paper.

Place the dates, cashews and salt in a food processor and pulse until the mixture gets difficult for the machine to continue to process. Add the dried blueberries and pulse until the blueberries are incorporated. Divide the mixture into 14 evenly sized portions, roll into balls and place them on the prepared baking sheet.

In a microwave-safe bowl, melt together the chocolate and coconut oil on 50 percent power in 15-second increments, stirring in between, until the chocolate is smooth. With a fork, dip each ball into the chocolate, let the excess chocolate drip off and then return the chocolate-covered ball to the baking sheet. Chill the balls in the freezer for 5 minutes or until the chocolate is solid. Drizzle the remaining chocolate over the balls and serve.

Crunchy Chocolate-Frosted Nut and Seed Bars gf

Seeded bars like these gluten-free crunchy bars are always on the top of my go-to snack list. Maybe it's the crunch or maybe it's the chocolate frosting (um, it's definitely the chocolate frosting!), but either way, you need these bars in your life!

Makes 16 bars

5 Medjool dates, pitted
5 tbsp (75 ml) maple syrup
1 cup (140 g) raw almonds
½ cup (60 g) roasted and salted pumpkin seeds
¼ cup (28 g) unsalted pistachios
½ cup (16 g) rice cereal (gluten free if necessary)
2 tbsp (14 g) flax meal
1 cup (180 g) vegan dark chocolate chips
1 tbsp (14 g) coconut oil

Preheat the oven to 350°F (180°C, or gas mark 4). Line two 8 x 4–inch (20 x 10–cm) loaf pans or one 8 x 8–inch (20 x 20–cm) pan with parchment paper, leaving some overhang so you can easily remove the bars.

Place the dates and maple syrup in a food processor or high-powered blender and blend until smooth, 1 to 2 minutes. Transfer the date paste to a large mixing bowl and add the almonds, pumpkin seeds, pistachios, rice cereal and flax meal. Use a rubber spatula to stir everything together until the date paste is well distributed.

Press the mixture into the bottom of the prepared pans and pack it as tightly as possible. Bake the bars for 20 to 25 minutes, until golden brown, checking every 10 to 15 minutes to make sure they don't burn. Remove the pans from the oven and let the bars cool completely.

In a microwave-safe bowl, melt together the chocolate chips and coconut oil on 50 percent power in 15-second increments, stirring in between, until the chocolate is smooth. Pour the chocolate on top of the bars and use a rubber spatula to spread it into an even layer. Place the pans in the refrigerator and chill the bars until the chocolate is solid.

Using the parchment-paper handles, remove the block from the pan and cut into 16 evenly sized bars.

Note: Store the bars in the refrigerator—they are delicious chilled!

Almond Butter Chocolate Date Balls gf

When you need a quick and easy snack that's made using only whole food ingredients, these almond butter date balls will do the trick. They are great for gatherings because they are gluten free and Paleo friendly.

Makes 12 balls

⅓ cup (85 g) natural almond butter

13 Medjool dates, pitted

½ cup (70 g) raw almonds

2 tbsp (10 g) Dutch-processed cocoa powder, plus more for dusting

1 tsp vanilla extract

Pinch of sea salt

Line a baking sheet with parchment paper.

Place all the ingredients in a food processor or high-powered blender and blend for 1 to 2 minutes, or until a ball begins to form. You will need to stop and scrape the sides as needed. Divide the dough into 12 evenly sized pieces, roll into balls and place them on the prepared baking sheet. Dust with cocoa powder and serve.

Note: Store the date balls in a sealed container. They are also great chilled in the fridge!

Secret Ingredient Brownie Batter Dip ⓖⓕ

Like the Cocoa-Swirled Meringue Cookies on page 29, in this recipe chickpeas take center stage! This is super easy to whip up and great for dipping—pretzels, strawberries, fresh fruit, crackers or anything that goes great with chocolate (which is pretty much *everything*, right?).

Serves 15

1 (15-oz [420-g]) can chickpeas, drained and rinsed

⅓ cup (80 ml) maple syrup

¼ cup (64 g) cashew butter

¼ tsp salt

½ tsp vanilla extract

¼ cup (20 g) unsweetened cocoa powder

¼ cup (60 ml) unsweetened almond milk

Vegan chocolate shavings, for topping

Place the chickpeas, maple syrup, cashew butter, salt, vanilla, cocoa powder and almond milk in a food processor or high-powered blender and blend on high speed for 2 to 3 minutes, stopping to scrape the sides as needed. Transfer to a serving dish and top with the chocolate shavings.

Chocolate Coconut Chia Pudding 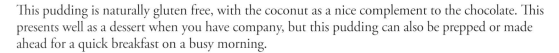 gf

This pudding is naturally gluten free, with the coconut as a nice complement to the chocolate. This presents well as a dessert when you have company, but this pudding can also be prepped or made ahead for a quick breakfast on a busy morning.

Serves 5

CHOCOLATE LAYER

3 tbsp (45 ml) maple syrup

3 tbsp (15 g) Dutch-processed cocoa powder

1 cup (240 ml) light coconut milk

⅛ tsp salt

1 tsp vanilla extract

⅓ cup (55 g) chia seeds

COCONUT LAYER

1 tbsp (15 ml) maple syrup

½ cup (120 ml) light coconut milk

½ tsp vanilla extract

Pinch of sea salt

2½ tbsp (25 g) chia seeds

TOPPINGS

Vegan chocolate shavings

Unsweetened shredded coconut, toasted

To make the chocolate layer, in a bowl, whisk together the maple syrup and cocoa powder until smooth. Add the coconut milk, salt and vanilla and whisk until combined. Add the chia seeds and stir until well combined. Cover the bowl with plastic wrap and chill in the refrigerator for 15 minutes.

To make the coconut layer, in a bowl, whisk together the maple syrup, coconut milk, vanilla and salt until smooth. Add the chia seeds and stir until well combined. Cover the bowl with plastic wrap and chill in the refrigerator for 15 minutes.

Remove the bowls from the refrigerator and stir both mixtures again to remove any clumps. Cover the bowls and chill the mixtures for at least 2 hours.

To assemble the puddings, divide the chocolate mixture among five serving glasses. Layer the coconut mixture on top. Finish the puddings with chocolate shavings and toasted coconut.

Chocolate Maple Granola ⬤gf

Ideal for early mornings accompanied with a big cup of coffee, this granola is a perfect way to start your day. Serve it with plant-based milk as a cereal, sprinkle it over a smoothie bowl or grab a handful and eat as an on-the-go snack. This granola keeps in an airtight container for up to 2 weeks.

Serves 8

2 cups (180 g) rolled oats (gluten free if necessary)

1 cup (110 g) slivered almonds

¾ cup (90 g) chopped hazelnuts

¼ cup (20 g) unsweetened cocoa powder

1 tbsp (10 g) chia seeds

¼ tsp sea salt

½ cup (93 g) quinoa, rinsed and cooked according to package directions

½ cup (120 g) coconut oil, melted

¼ cup (60 ml) maple syrup

1 tsp vanilla extract

⅓ cup (60 g) chopped vegan chocolate

Fresh blueberries, for garnish (optional)

Preheat the oven to 325°F (165°C, or gas mark 3) and line a baking sheet with parchment paper.

In a large bowl, combine the oats, almonds, hazelnuts, cocoa powder, chia seeds and sea salt.

In another bowl, whisk together the cooked quinoa, coconut oil, maple syrup and vanilla until combined. Add the wet ingredients to the dry ingredients and stir with a wooden spoon or spatula until all the ingredients are well coated and no dry bits remain.

Transfer the mixture to the prepared baking sheet and spread it in an even layer. Bake for 10 minutes. Stir the granola from the edges (which will brown faster) to the center and spread in an even layer. Bake for 4 to 5 minutes, or until the granola is evenly golden brown.

Remove the baking sheet from the oven and let the granola cool completely, about 30 minutes. Add the chopped chocolate and stir to combine. Top with fresh blueberries, if desired.

Note: The granola will harden as it cools.

Chocolate for breakfast

If you can have chocolate chip cookies for dinner, then you can surely have chocolate for breakfast! When I gave in to the urge of having treats for breakfast, my mind raced with ideas. I started having dreams about Chocolate Hazelnut–Stuffed French Toast (page 124) and crepes filled with gobs of chocolate hazelnut spread and strawberries (page 123).

I wholeheartedly believe in eating chocolate the first thing in the morning. A good start is important to me, and it builds a foundation for a great day. And I know it's going to be a great day when it starts with a plate of Banana Chocolate Chip Pancakes (page 119).

Chocolate Chip Orange Waffles

With the right balance, chocolate and citrus complement each other perfectly. These crunchy chocolate chip waffles have a hint of orange citrus, adding a little zest to a hearty breakfast staple. These are amazing with or without maple syrup.

Serves 6

2 cups (240 g) all-purpose flour or gluten-free baking flour

⅓ cup (30 g) unsweetened cocoa powder

2 tbsp (24 g) granulated sugar

1½ tsp (4 g) baking powder

¼ tsp salt

¼ cup (60 ml) vegetable oil

1¾ cups (420 ml) almond milk

1 tbsp (15 ml) orange juice

1 tbsp (6 g) orange zest

¼ cup (45 g) mini vegan chocolate chips

In a mixing bowl, stir together the flour, cocoa powder, sugar, baking powder and salt until combined. Add the oil, almond milk, orange juice and zest and mix until no lumps are visible, about 30 seconds. Fold in the chocolate chips.

Prepare a standard size waffle iron with nonstick spray and set over high heat. Pour ⅓ cup (80 ml) of the batter into the center of the iron, close the iron and cook for 2 to 4 minutes, until crispy. Repeat until you have used all the batter.

Banana Chocolate Chip Pancakes

Blueberries, raspberries and strawberries are great. But I like my pancakes with small bursts of chocolate and hints of banana. Over the years, I've perfected the balance of ingredients to suit my taste with these delicious chocolate chip banana pancakes. I hope they become your faves too!

Serves 3

1 cup (120 g) all-purpose flour

1 tsp baking soda

¼ cup (45 g) vegan mini chocolate chips

1 banana, mashed (½ cup [112 g])

2 tbsp (30 g) coconut oil, melted

2 tbsp (30 ml) maple syrup

1 cup (240 ml) almond milk or plant-based milk of choice

2 tsp (10 ml) distilled white vinegar

½ tsp vanilla extract

OPTIONAL TOPPINGS

Sliced banana

Vegan chocolate chips

Maple syrup

In a large mixing bowl, stir together the flour, baking soda and chocolate chips. In another bowl, stir together the mashed banana, coconut oil, maple syrup, almond milk, vinegar and vanilla until smooth. Add the wet ingredients to the dry ingredients and stir until no dry spots remain.

Coat a large nonstick skillet or pancake pan with nonstick spray, heat it over medium-low heat and then pour ⅓ cup (80 ml) of the batter for each pancake into the pan. Cook the pancakes for 2½ minutes, or until the edges start to brown and bubbles begin to form, then flip the pancakes and cook the other side for 1 minute. Serve hot with any or all of the optional toppings, if desired.

Peanut Butter–Swirled Chocolate Muffins

It's no secret that I *love* peanut butter. Peanut butter–swirled muffins were a no-brainer when I was trying to decide on my recipes for this book. Also, do you like how I disguised this cupcake as "breakfast"? ;)

Makes 12 muffins

2 tbsp (14 g) flax meal

6 tbsp (90 ml) water

1½ cups (180 g) all-purpose flour

½ cup (40 g) unsweetened cocoa powder

1 tsp baking powder

½ tsp baking soda

½ cup (90 g) vegan chocolate chunks, plus more for topping

½ cup (113 g) vegan butter, at room temperature

½ cup (110 g) packed brown sugar

¼ cup (50 g) granulated sugar

1 tsp vanilla extract

¾ cup (180 ml) almond milk

¾ cup (185 g) natural peanut butter

Preheat the oven to 350°F (180°C, or gas mark 4) and line a muffin pan with 12 cupcake liners.

In a small bowl, stir together the flax meal and water and then set it aside to gel, about 5 minutes.

In a medium bowl, stir together the flour, cocoa powder, baking powder and baking soda until combined. Stir in the chocolate chunks.

In a large bowl using an electric mixer, beat the butter, brown sugar and granulated sugar until creamy, about 1 minute. Add the vanilla and flax mixture and beat until well blended, about 1 minute. Add the almond milk and mix until smooth. Slowly add the dry ingredients and mix just until combined. Try not to overmix the batter.

Evenly divide the batter among the muffin liners. Drop dollops of peanut butter (about 1 tablespoon [15 g]) over the batter and use a sharp knife to swirl the peanut butter and batter together, then top with more chocolate chunks. Bake the muffins for 18 to 20 minutes, or until the tops of the muffins spring back immediately when touched with your finger.

Remove the muffins from the pan and let them cool before serving.

Strawberry Chocolate Hazelnut Crepes

Crepes filled with hazelnut spread and fresh strawberries are a match made in heaven! I love these freshly made, but they are also delicious as tomorrow's snack, chilled in the fridge.

Serves 6

STRAWBERRY FILLING

½ cup (83 g) chopped strawberries

1 tsp lemon juice

1 tsp granulated sugar

CREPES

2 cups (240 g) all-purpose flour

1½ tsp (5 g) tapioca flour

⅛ tsp salt

2 tbsp (30 ml) maple syrup

2 cups (480 ml) almond milk

1 tsp vanilla extract

½ cup (150 g) vegan chocolate hazelnut spread

To make the filling, in a small bowl, stir together the strawberries, lemon juice and sugar; set aside.

To make the crepes, in a large bowl, stir together the flour, tapioca flour and salt until combined. Add the maple syrup, almond milk and vanilla and whisk until no lumps remain, 1 to 2 minutes.

Coat a large frying pan or crepe pan with nonstick spray and set it over medium-low heat. Once the pan is heated, hold it just above the heat and add ¾ cup (180 ml) of the batter to the center of the pan. Immediately swirl the pan in a circular motion so the batter spreads out into a thin layer and coats the pan evenly. Cook the crepe for 1 minute. The edges should start to pull away when it's ready. Gently loosen the crepe with a spatula and flip. Cook for 20 to 30 seconds on the other side. Slide the crepe out of the pan onto a plate and repeat the process until you have used all the batter.

Fill the crepes with 1 to 2 tablespoons (18 to 36 g) of the hazelnut spread and top with the strawberry mixture.

Chocolate Hazelnut–Stuffed French Toast

French toast gets a makeover—my version has chocolate (of course!) and hazelnut stuffed into every bite. Add some bananas and a little maple syrup, and you have a delicious treat for breakfast or brunch!

Serves 4

1 cup (240 ml) almond milk

1 tbsp (7 g) flax meal

1 tbsp (15 ml) maple syrup

1 tsp vanilla extract

½ tsp ground cinnamon

¼ cup (70 g) vegan chocolate hazelnut spread

4 slices sourdough bread (or any crusty bread)

3 tbsp (22 g) finely chopped chocolate

TOPPINGS

Sliced banana

Confectioners' sugar, for dusting

Maple syrup

In a large and shallow bowl, whisk together the almond milk, flax meal, maple syrup, vanilla and cinnamon and then set it aside for 15 minutes for the flax to gel.

Meanwhile, spread 1 tablespoon (18 g) of hazelnut spread onto one side of each slice of bread and sprinkle the chopped chocolate over it. Put the slices together to create two sandwiches. Dip each sandwich in the almond milk mixture and make sure it's well coated.

Coat a nonstick pan with nonstick spray and set it over medium-low heat. Place the sandwiches in the hot pan and cook them for 2 to 3 minutes on each side, or until golden brown. Cut the sandwiches in half, top with sliced bananas, dust with confectioners' sugar and drizzle with maple syrup. Serve immediately.

Chocolate Strawberry Oat Scones gf

I adore scones and I try to make a batch once a month or so because they go so well with my coffee, especially on a busy morning. The chocolate chunks and strawberry bits make a perfect combination.

Makes 6 scones

SCONES

1 tbsp (7 g) flax meal

3 tbsp (45 ml) water

1¾ cups (210 g) all-purpose flour or gluten-free baking flour

1 cup (80 g) rolled oats (gluten free if necessary)

½ cup (100 g) granulated sugar

1½ tsp (4 g) baking powder

⅛ tsp salt

½ cup (90 g) chopped vegan chocolate

½ cup (113) vegan butter, melted and cooled

⅓ cup (80 ml) almond milk

1 tsp lemon juice

1 tsp vanilla extract

1 cup (150 g) frozen strawberries, chopped

GLAZE

¾ cup (90 g) confectioners' sugar, sifted

2 tbsp (30 ml) almond milk

Preheat the oven to 425°F (220°C, or gas mark 7) and line a baking sheet with parchment paper.

To make the scones, in a small bowl, stir together the flax meal and water and then set it aside to gel, about 5 minutes.

In a large bowl, stir together the flour, rolled oats, sugar, baking powder, salt and chocolate until combined.

In a medium bowl, whisk together the melted butter, almond milk, lemon juice and vanilla. Add the flax mixture and whisk to combine. Pour the wet mixture over the dry ingredients and stir until a dough forms. Remove the frozen strawberries from the freezer and carefully fold them into the dough. Turn the dough out onto a floured surface and pat into a 1-inch (2.5-cm)-thick square. Cut the dough into 6 evenly sized squares and place them on the prepared baking sheet. Bake the scones for 16 to 18 minutes, until golden brown. Remove the scones from the oven and let cool on a rack.

To make the glaze, in a small bowl, stir together the confectioners' sugar and almond milk and drizzle the glaze over the scones.

Marbled Chocolate Banana Loaf

When you can't choose between classic banana bread and chocolate—why not have both? What's even better is that it's gluten free as well! This soft, tender bread gets better with age. Keep this loaf, covered, for up to 1 week. It's great with ice cream, too.

Serves 10

BANANA LAYER

1 tbsp (7 g) flax meal

2 tbsp (30 ml) water

3 overly ripe medium bananas (about 1½ cups [225 g])

½ cup (120 g) coconut oil, softened

¾ cup (165 g) packed brown sugar

½ cup (120 ml) almond milk

1 tsp vanilla extract

1 tsp distilled white vinegar

1 tbsp (9 g) tapioca flour

2 cups (240 g) all-purpose flour or gluten-free baking flour

1 tsp baking soda

½ tsp baking powder

¼ tsp salt

CHOCOLATE LAYER

¼ cup (20 g) unsweetened cocoa powder

¼ cup (60 ml) almond milk

1 tbsp (14 g) coconut oil, melted

GLAZE

¾ cup (135 g) vegan chocolate chips

½ tsp coconut oil

Preheat the oven to 350°F (180°C, or gas mark 4). Coat a 9 x 5–inch (23 x 13–cm) loaf pan with coconut oil and line the bottom with parchment paper.

To make the banana layer, in a small bowl, stir together the flax meal and water and then set it aside to gel for about 5 minutes.

Meanwhile, in a blender, blend together the bananas, coconut oil, brown sugar, almond milk, vanilla and vinegar until smooth, about 30 seconds. Add the flax mixture and blend until smooth. Transfer the mixture to a large mixing bowl. Add the flours, baking soda, baking powder and salt and stir with a rubber spatula just until the batter is combined and no dry bits remain. Divide the batter between two bowls.

To make the chocolate layer, in one of the bowls, add the cocoa powder, almond milk and coconut oil and stir until smooth.

Spoon about ¼ cup (60 ml) of the chocolate mixture into the prepared pan and spread it out to cover the bottom. Top the chocolate mixture with the plain banana batter and then repeat this process until you have used all the batter. Bake the loaf for 60 to 65 minutes, or until a toothpick comes out clean. Remove the pan from the oven and let the cake cool, then turn it out of the pan and peel off the parchment paper.

To make the glaze, in a microwave-safe bowl, melt together the chocolate chips and coconut oil on 50 percent power in 20-second increments, stirring in between, until smooth. Pour the glaze over the loaf and let the chocolate set before serving.

Easy Chocolate Chia Overnight Oats

Who says you can't have chocolate for breakfast? Prep these chocolate chia overnight oats two days before, the night before, or even an hour before. They are happy and content in the fridge, ready for action whenever you are!

Serves 2

1 cup (80 g) rolled oats (gluten free if necessary)

¼ cup (30 g) slivered almonds

2½ tbsp (12 g) unsweetened cocoa powder

1 tbsp (10 g) chia seeds

⅛ tsp salt

1¼ cups (300 ml) unsweetened almond or plant-based milk of choice

2 tbsp (30 ml) maple syrup

1 tbsp (11 g) vegan mini chocolate chips

In a mixing bowl, stir together the oats, almonds, cocoa powder, chia seeds and salt until combined. Add the almond milk and maple syrup and stir until no dry spots remain. Cover the bowl with plastic wrap and chill in the refrigerator for 30 minutes, or until ready to serve. Top with the chocolate chips before serving.

Chocolate Quinoa Breakfast Bowl gf

I love oatmeal, but sometimes it's nice to change it up a bit. How about swapping it with a healthy and nourishing quinoa breakfast infused with rich chocolate? I like mine with bananas or raspberries (or both!), but the choice of toppings is practically endless.

Serves 2

½ cup (90 g) quinoa

1¼ cups (300 ml) almond milk, divided

2 tbsp (10 g) Dutch-processed cocoa powder

2 tbsp (30 ml) maple syrup

TOPPINGS

Banana slices

Vegan chocolate

Raspberries

. . . or anything you want!

In a fine-mesh strainer, rinse the quinoa well until the water runs clear. Place 1 cup (240 ml) of the almond milk, cocoa powder and maple syrup in a small pot over medium-high heat and whisk until smooth. Add the quinoa and stir until combined. Bring the mixture to a boil, lower the heat and simmer for 10 minutes. Watch it carefully so that it doesn't boil over. Remove the pot from the heat, cover the pot and let sit for 5 to 10 minutes.

Add the remaining ¼ cup (60 ml) of almond milk, fluff the quinoa with a fork and transfer the mixture to serving bowls. Add your toppings of choice and enjoy!

Elvis Peanut Butter Banana Donuts

The great Elvis Presley famously loved his fried peanut butter and banana sandwiches—and it's rumored that he fried them in bacon grease or even included bacon in the sandwich itself! This recipe is an homage to the King, but safe for vegans. These banana bread donuts are peanut butter flavored—baked, not fried—and topped with a rich chocolate glaze.

Makes 9 donuts

DONUTS

1 tbsp (7 g) flax meal

3 tbsp (45 ml) water

2 overly ripe bananas, mashed (about 1 cup [236 g])

2 tbsp (30 g) coconut oil, melted

¼ cup (64 g) natural peanut butter

½ cup (110 g) packed brown sugar

¼ cup (60 ml) almond milk

1 tsp vanilla extract

1 tsp distilled white vinegar

1⅓ cups (160 g) all-purpose flour

1 tbsp (9 g) tapioca flour

1 tsp baking soda

½ tsp baking powder

¼ tsp salt

TOPPING

1½ cups (270 g) vegan chocolate chips

2 tsp (10 g) coconut oil

3 vegan peanut butter cups, chopped

Preheat the oven to 350°F (180°C, or gas mark 4). Coat 9 molds of a standard donut pan with nonstick spray.

To make the donuts, in a small bowl, stir together the flax meal and water until combined and then set it aside to gel, about 5 minutes.

In a large bowl, whisk together the mashed bananas, coconut oil, peanut butter, brown sugar, almond milk, vanilla and vinegar until smooth, about 1 minute. Add the flax mixture and whisk until blended.

In a medium bowl, stir together the all-purpose flour, tapioca flour, baking soda, baking powder and salt. Gradually add the dry ingredients to the wet and stir just until combined and no dry spots remain.

Transfer the batter to a piping bag and fill the prepared 9 donut molds with batter. Bake the donuts for 19 to 22 minutes, until a toothpick inserted near the center comes out clean. Let the donuts cool in the pan for 10 minutes, then remove them from the pan and transfer them to a rack to continue cooling for 20 minutes.

To make the topping, in a microwave-safe bowl, melt together the chocolate and coconut oil on 50 percent power until melted and smooth, about 1 minute. Dip the tops of each donut in the chocolate and let the excess drip off. Sprinkle with the chopped peanut butter cups. Let the donuts sit at room temperature for 1 hour or chill in the refrigerator for 10 minutes so the chocolate hardens before serving.

Streusel-Topped Double Chocolate Banana Muffins

Why eat an ordinary chocolate muffin when you can have one with crunchy streusel? Incredibly rich but not overly sweet, these muffins have just the right balance of cake and crunch. Serving them with a cup of coffee is a must!

Makes 12 muffins

MUFFINS

2 tbsp (14 g) flax meal

6 tbsp (90 ml) water

1½ cups (180 g) all-purpose flour

1 cup (80 g) rolled oats

½ cup (100 g) granulated sugar

5 tbsp (25 g) unsweetened cocoa powder

2 tsp (6 g) baking powder

1 tsp baking soda

¼ tsp salt

3 overly ripe large bananas (about 1½ cups [225 g])

5 tbsp (75 g) coconut oil, melted

¼ cup (60 ml) almond milk

1 tsp vanilla extract

½ cup (90 g) vegan chocolate chips

STREUSEL TOPPING

¼ cup (30 g) all-purpose flour

3 tbsp (42 g) packed brown sugar

1 tbsp (14 g) vegan butter, at room temperature

¼ cup (45 g) vegan chocolate chips

Preheat the oven to 400°F (200°C, or gas mark 6) and line a muffin tin with liners.

To make the muffins, in a small bowl, stir together the flax meal and water and then set it aside to gel, about 5 minutes.

In a medium bowl, stir together the flour, rolled oats, granulated sugar, cocoa powder, baking powder, baking soda and salt until combined.

In a large bowl, use a fork to mash the bananas. Add the flax mixture, coconut oil, almond milk and vanilla and mix until smooth and combined. Pour the dry ingredients into the wet ingredients and stir with a rubber spatula just until no dry spots remain. Try not to overmix the batter. Fold in the chocolate chips. Use a cookie scooper to fill the cupcake liners about three-fourths of the way full.

To make the topping, in a bowl, stir together the flour and brown sugar. Add the butter and cut it into the flour using a fork or pastry cutter until sandy crumbles form. Sprinkle the streusel on top of the muffins and then sprinkle with the chocolate chips. Bake the muffins for 18 to 22 minutes, until a toothpick inserted in the center comes out clean. Let the muffins cool before serving.

Double Chocolate Sweet Rolls

Super rich, super tasty and super chocolatey, these sweet rolls are extra special because they aren't just filled with chocolate but topped with chocolate too! They're made with self-rising flour, so there's no yeast and no rising time required to make this sweet treat.

Makes 8 rolls

ROLLS

2½ cups (300 g) self-rising flour, plus more for dusting

3 tbsp (36 g) granulated sugar

2 tbsp (28 g) vegan butter, melted, plus more for brushing

1 cup (240 ml) almond milk

1 tsp vanilla extract

FILLING

¼ cup (56 g) vegan butter, at room temperature

2 tbsp (25 g) packed brown sugar

2 tbsp (10 g) Dutch-processed cocoa powder

GLAZE

½ cup (90 g) vegan dark chocolate chips

1 tsp coconut oil

Preheat the oven to 350°F (180°C, or gas mark 4) and line a baking sheet with parchment paper.

To make the rolls, in a large bowl, stir together the flour and granulated sugar. In a medium bowl, stir together the melted butter, almond milk and vanilla. Add the wet ingredients to the dry ingredients and use a rubber spatula to stir them together until a soft dough forms and no dry bits remain, 1 to 2 minutes.

Transfer the dough to a clean and generously floured surface. Sprinkle more flour over the dough and knead until the dough is smooth, 5 or 6 folds. Dust a rolling pin with flour and roll the dough into a 12 x 8–inch (30 x 20–cm) rectangle about ¼ inch (6 mm) thick with the shorter side facing you.

To make the filling, in a small bowl using an electric mixer, beat the butter until light and fluffy, about 1 minute. Add the brown sugar and cocoa powder and beat until well combined. Spread the filling in an even layer over the dough, leaving a ½-inch (1.3-cm) border around the edges. Fold the bottom two-thirds of the dough up and then fold the remaining top over the bottom fold, like an envelope.

Slice the dough perpendicular to the folded side into eight 1-inch (2.5-cm) strips. Carefully remove a strip and twist it about five turns. Take the bottom of the twisted strip and pull it up and around the top, and then tuck the end pieces under. (This process is messy but worth it!) Carefully transfer the twisted and tucked roll to the prepared baking sheet. Repeat until you have twisted and tucked all the strips. Brush the rolls with melted butter and bake them for 12 to 14 minutes, until golden brown. Remove the baking sheet from the oven and let the rolls cool slightly.

To make the glaze, in a microwave-safe bowl, melt together the chocolate and coconut oil on 50 percent power in 20-second increments, stirring in between, until smooth. Drizzle the chocolate over the warm rolls and then serve immediately.

Acknowledgments

To my fiancé, Daniel, you have been my rock. Thank you for your unconditional love and encouragement.

To my mom, who taught me that eating cookie dough at midnight is completely acceptable behavior. Who knew I would make a career out of it? Thank you for always supporting me in all my endeavors.

To my dad, who taught me that boredom sparks creativity. Thank you for always pushing me to try something new and not to be scared of failing.

Thank you to Michael Boezi, for all your incredible help editing and organizing during the writing process. I am forever grateful for your hard work and friendship!

If I could, I would give everyone at Page Street Publishing a hug and thank them personally for helping me create this book. Emily Taylor, I feel so fortunate for the opportunity to work with you and the entire Page Street team!

Also, thank you to all my family and friends for your endless support during the creation of this book. You have helped me make Peanut Butter Plus Chocolate what it is today.

Finally, a HUGE thank you to all my Peanut Butter Plus Chocolate followers from Instagram to the blog, for your endless support, encouragement and inspiration. I've learned so much from my fellow food bloggers and I am inspired by your work every single day. Thank you for always being my cheerleaders!

About the Author

Ciarra Siller is an actor, a recipe creator, a food photographer and founder of Peanut Butter Plus Chocolate, a recipe resource with not just chocolate recipes but also a variety of desserts that serve many different dietary needs. Ciarra's recipes and photos have been featured on feedfeed, as well as in multiple issues and on the cover of *Thrive* magazine. Learn more at www.peanutbutterpluschocolate.com or on Instagram @peanutbutterpluschocolate.

Index

T

W

Z